FOR ORGANS, PIANOS & ELECTRONIC KEYBOARDS

E-Z PLAY® TODAY

309

3-Chord Rock 'n' Roll

ISBN 978-0-634-07040-2

HAL•LEONARD®
CORPORATION
7777 W. BLUEMOUND RD. P.O. BOX 13819 MILWAUKEE, WI 53213

Visit Hal Leonard Online at
www.halleonard.com

All Shook Up

Registration 5
Rhythm: Rock

Words and Music by Otis Blackwell
and Elvis Presley

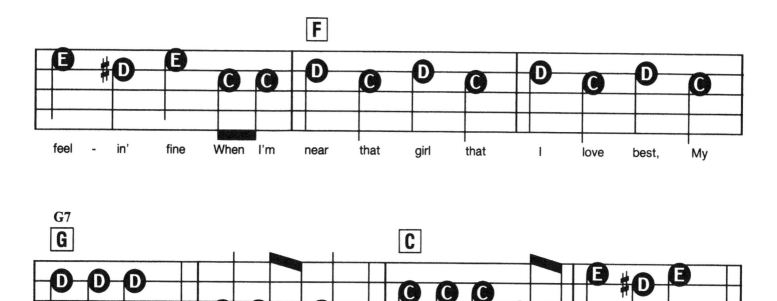

feel - in' fine When I'm near that girl that I love best, My

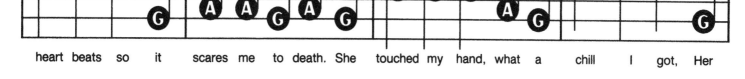

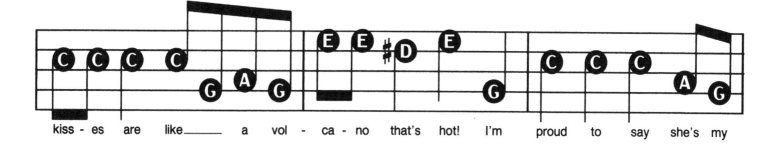

heart beats so it scares me to death. She touched my hand, what a chill I got, Her

kiss - es are like_____ a vol - ca - no that's hot! I'm proud to say she's my

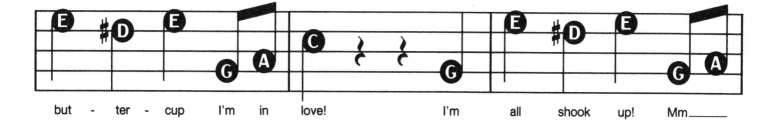

but - ter - cup I'm in love! I'm all shook up! Mm_____

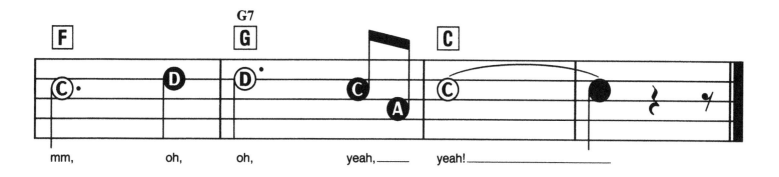

mm, oh, oh, yeah,_____ yeah!_____

Barbara Ann

Registration 7
Rhythm: Rock

Words and Music by
Fred Fassert

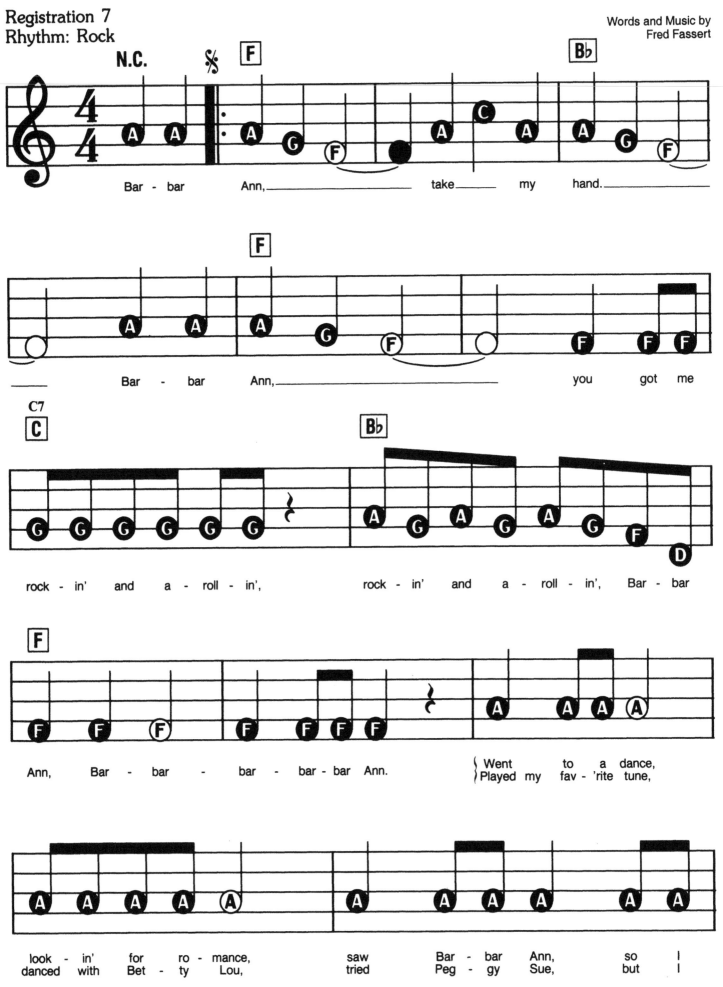

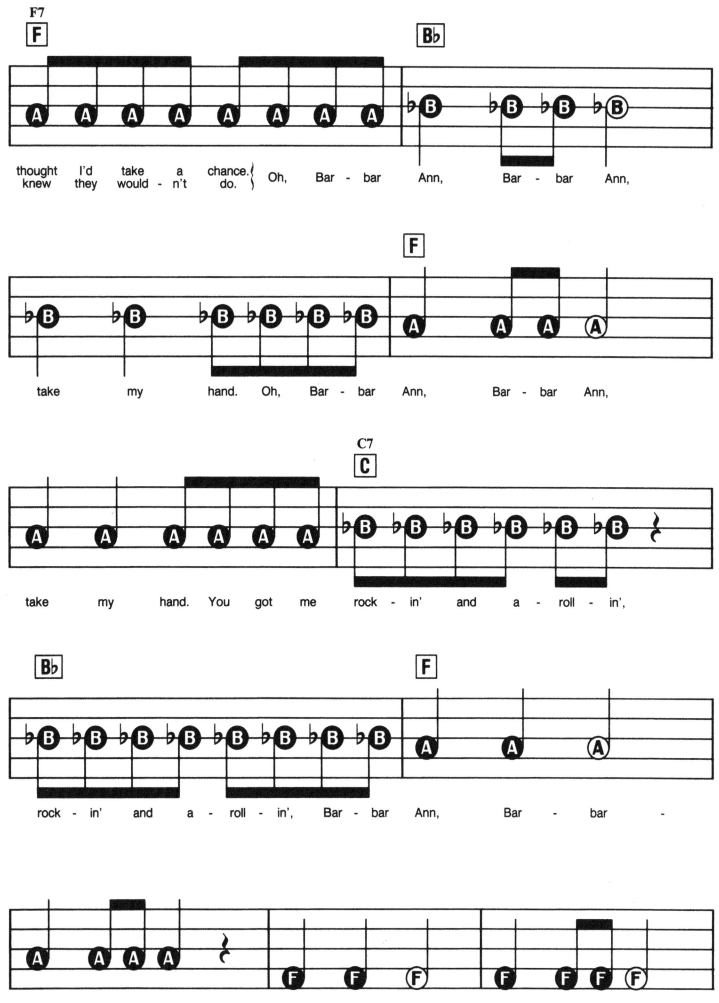

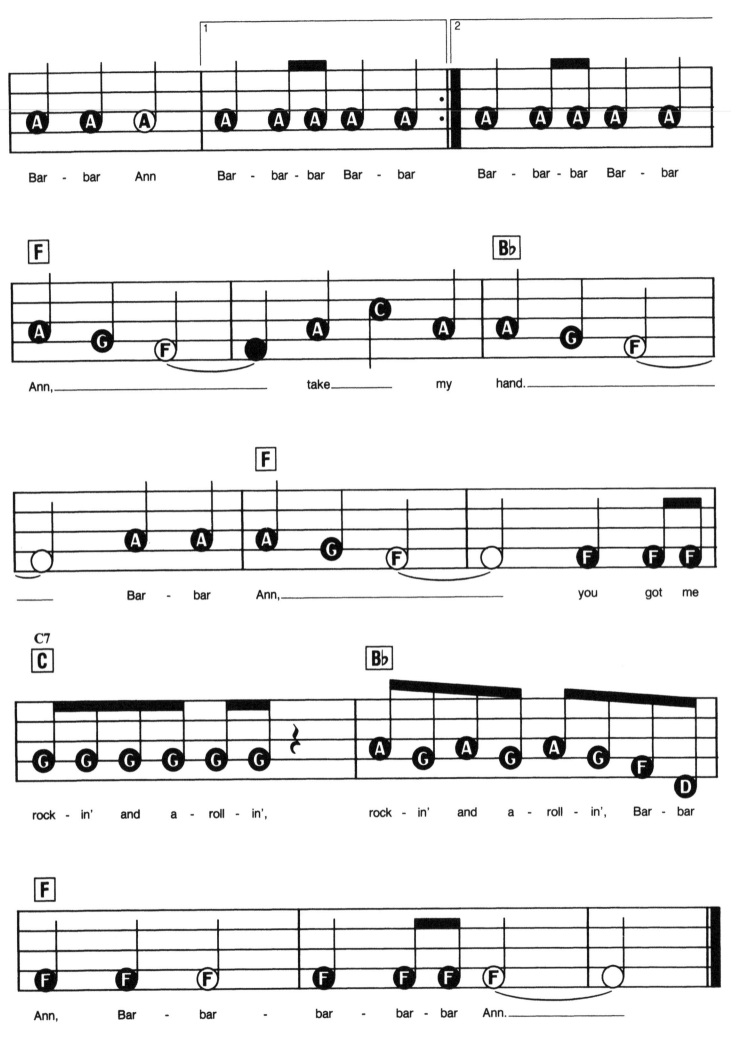

Bar - bar Ann   Bar - bar - bar Bar - bar   Bar - bar - bar Bar - bar

Ann,_____ take_____ my hand._____

_____ Bar - bar Ann,_____ you got me

rock - in' and a - roll - in',   rock - in' and a - roll - in', Bar - bar

Ann, Bar - bar - bar - bar - bar Ann._____

Be-Bop-A-Lula

Registration 8
Rhythm: Rock 'n' Roll or Shuffle

Words and Music by Tex Davis
and Gene Vincent

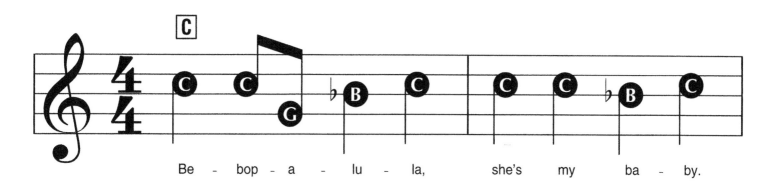

Be - bop - a - lu - la, she's my ba - by.

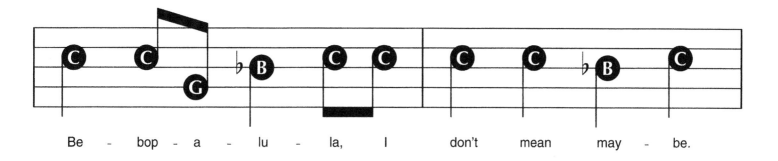

Be - bop - a - lu - la, I don't mean may - be.

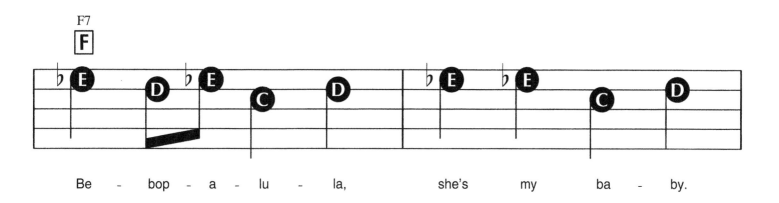

Be - bop - a - lu - la, she's my ba - by.

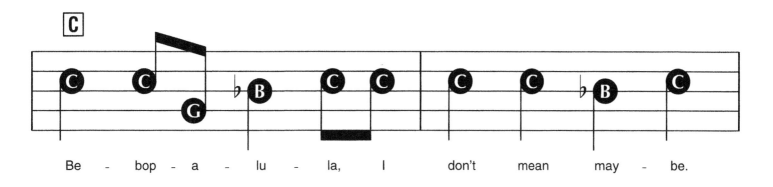

Be - bop - a - lu - la, I don't mean may - be.

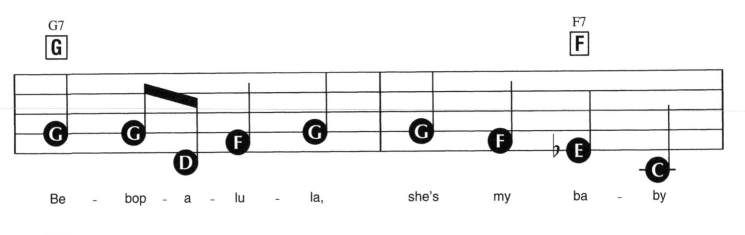

Be - bop - a - lu - la, she's my ba - by

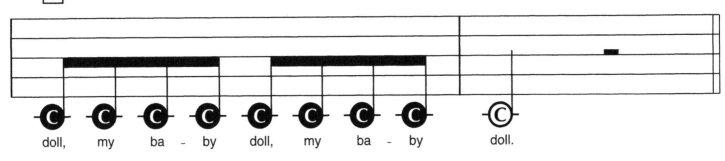

doll, my ba - by doll, my ba - by doll.

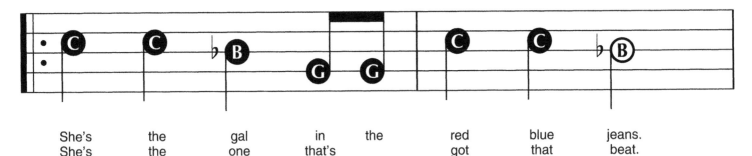

She's the gal in the red blue jeans.
She's the one that's got that beat.

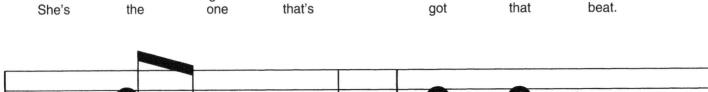

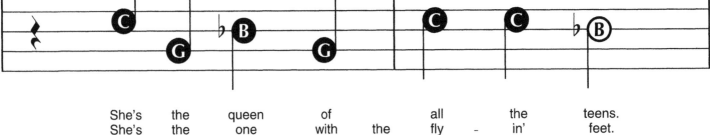

She's the queen of all the teens.
She's the one with the fly - in' feet.

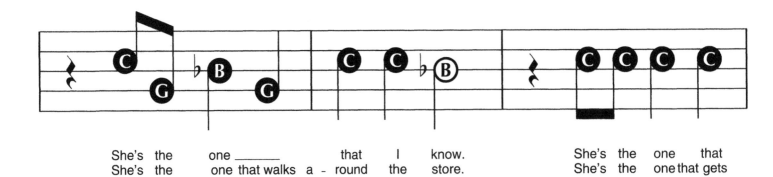

She's the one ____ that I know.
She's the one that walks a - round the store.

She's the one that
She's the one that gets

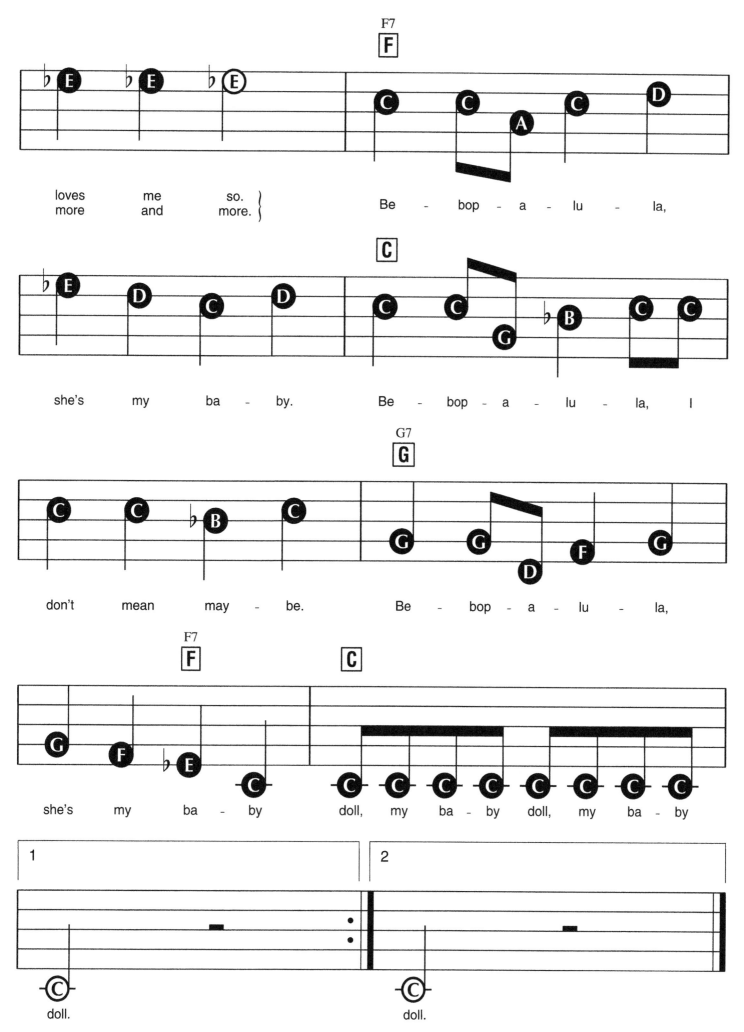

Blue Suede Shoes

Registration 2
Rhythm: Rock

Words and Music by
Carl Lee Perkins

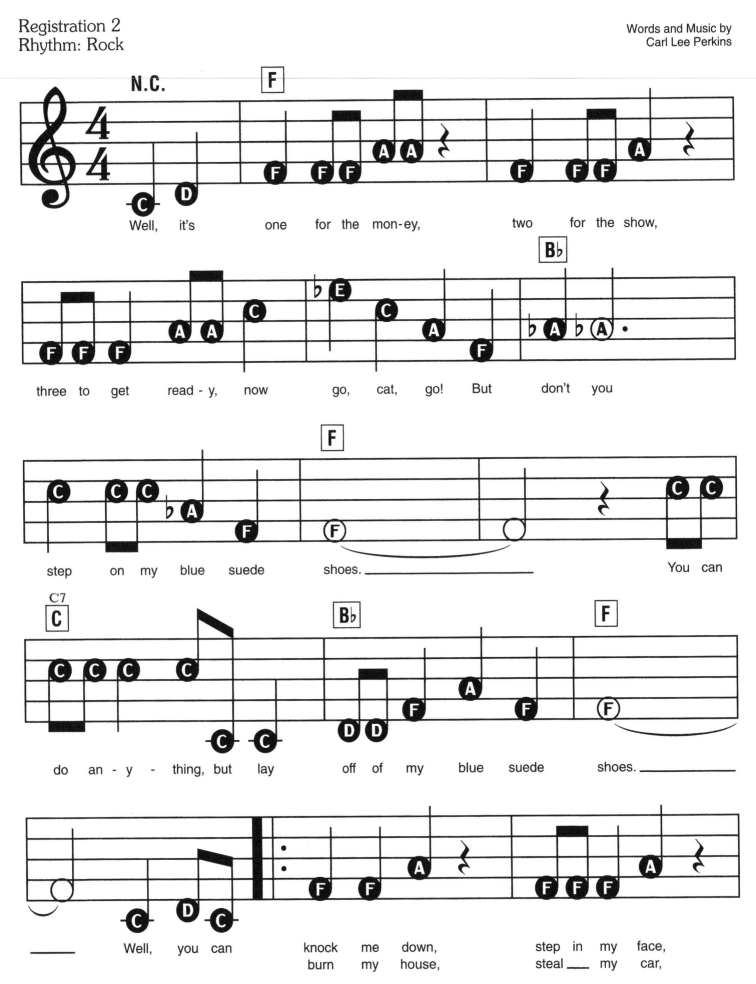

13

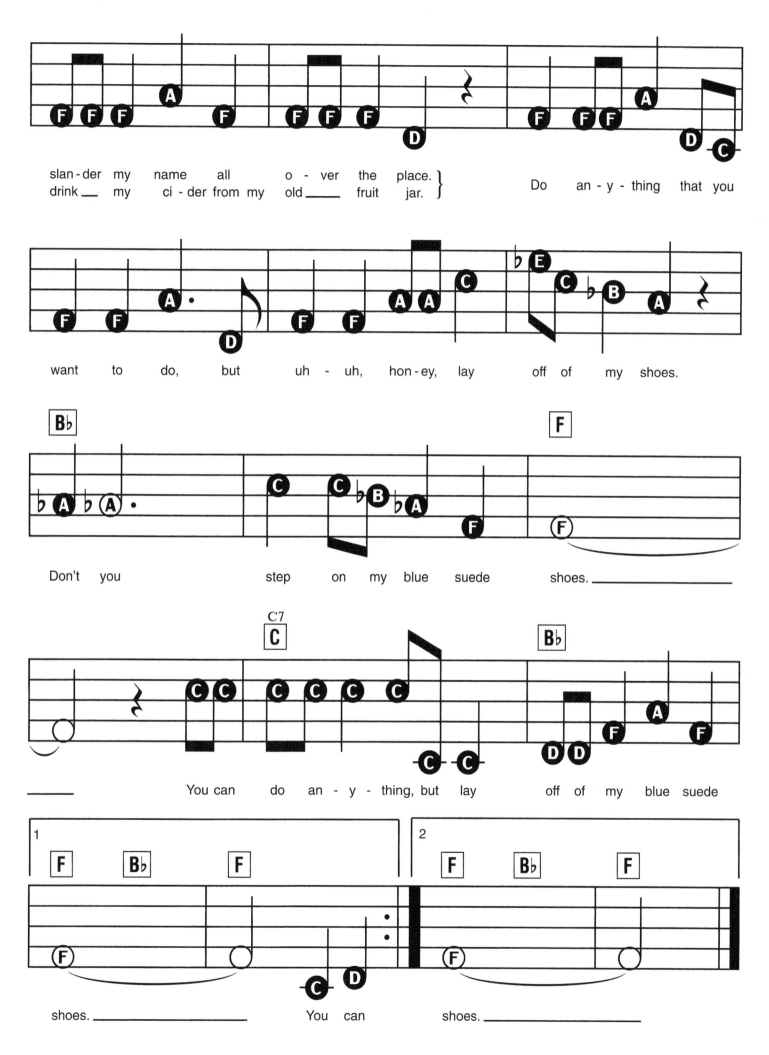

Bye Bye Love

Registration 4
Rhythm: Fox Trot or Swing

Words and Music by Felice Bryant
and Boudleaux Bryant

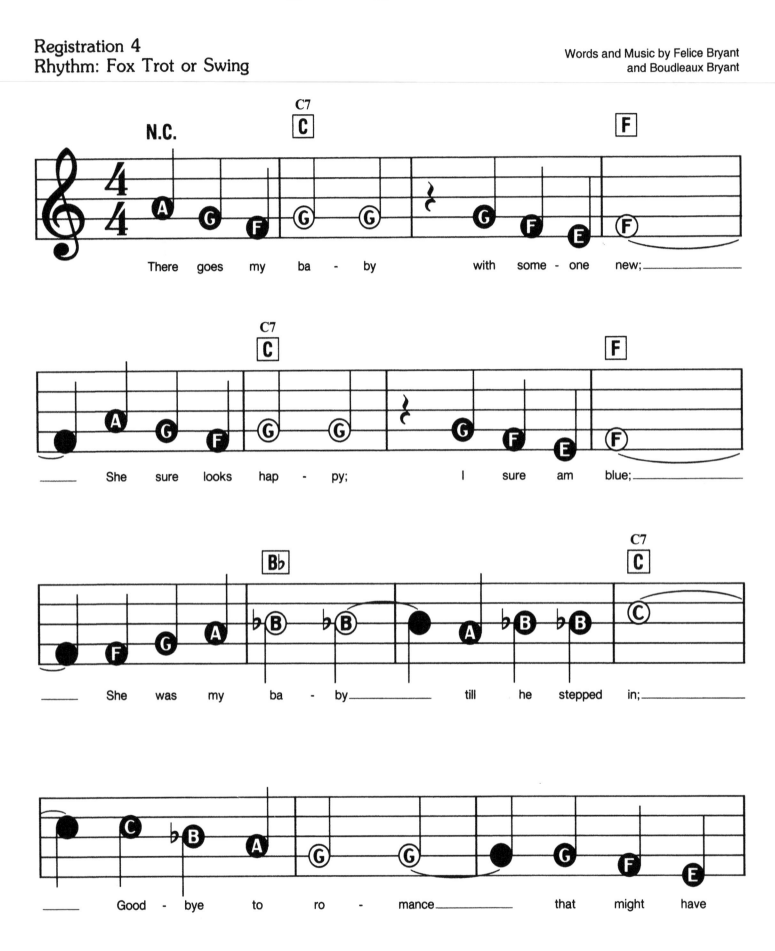

Do Wah Diddy Diddy

Registration 5
Rhythm: Rock or Pops

Words and Music by Jeff Barry
and Ellie Greenwich

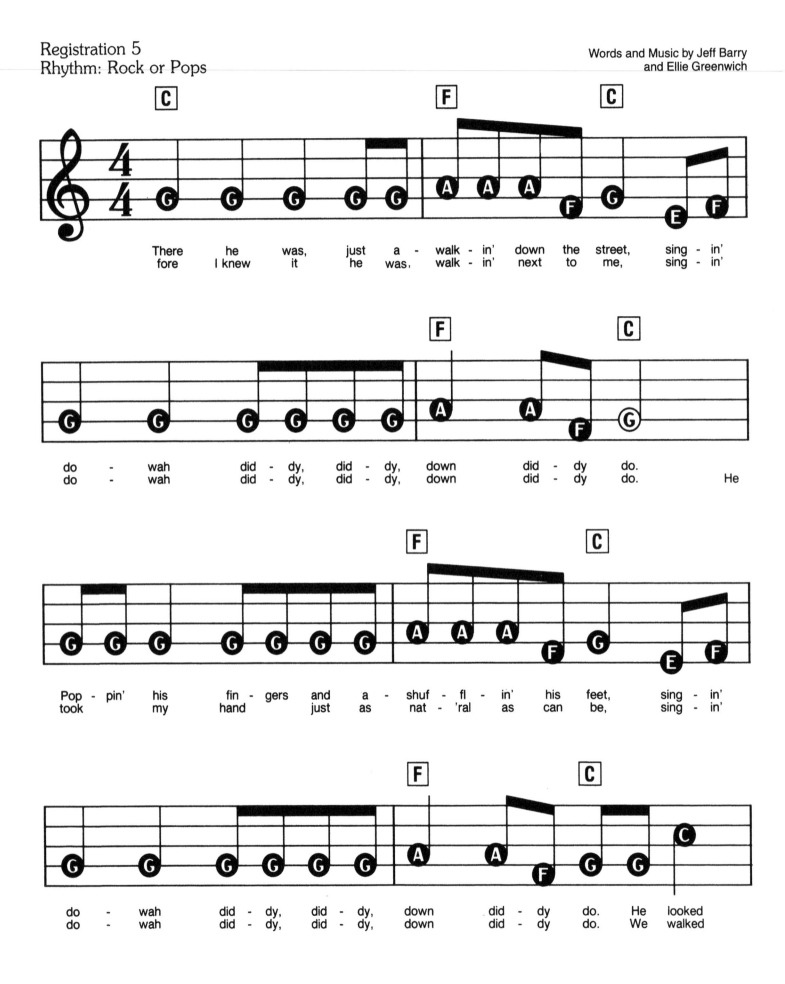

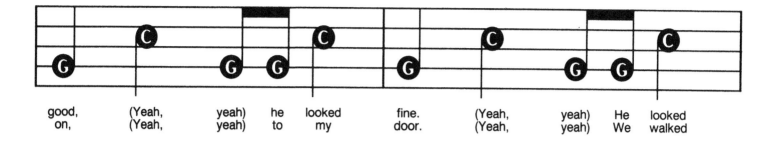

good, (Yeah, yeah) he looked fine. (Yeah, yeah) He looked
on, (Yeah, yeah) to looked my door. (Yeah, yeah) We walked

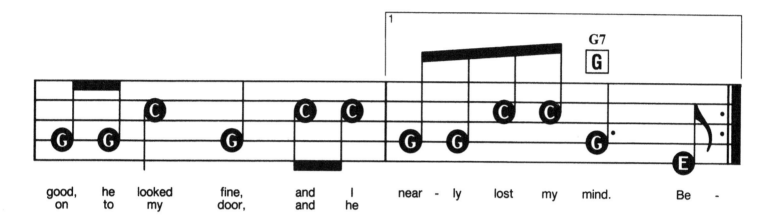

good, he looked fine, and I near - ly lost my mind. Be -
on to my door, and and he

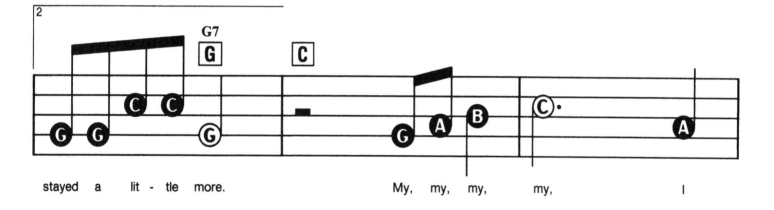

stayed a lit - tle more. My, my, my, my, I

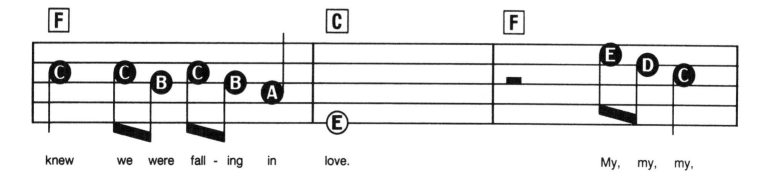

knew we were fall - ing in love. My, my, my,

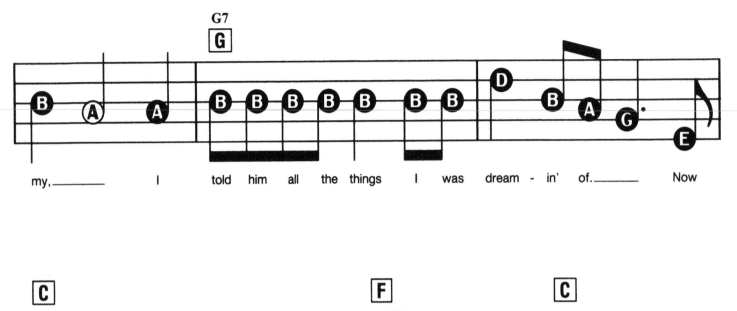

my,_____ I told him all the things I was dream - in' of._____ Now

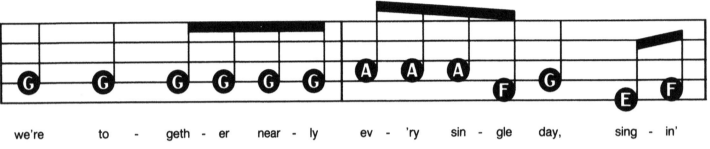

we're to - geth - er near - ly ev - 'ry sin - gle day, sing - in'

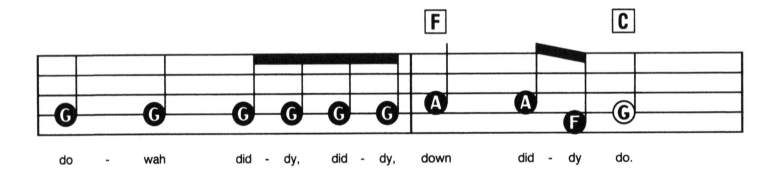

do - wah did - dy, did - dy, down did - dy do.

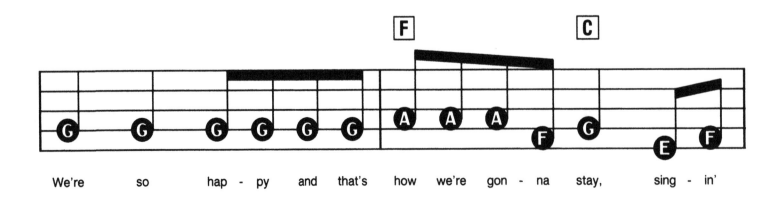

We're so hap - py and that's how we're gon - na stay, sing - in'

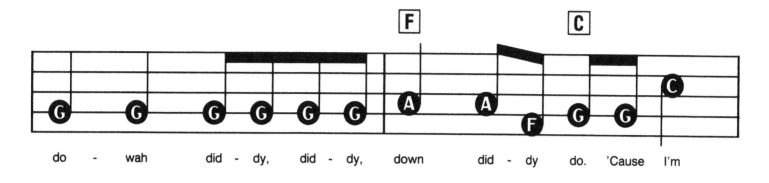

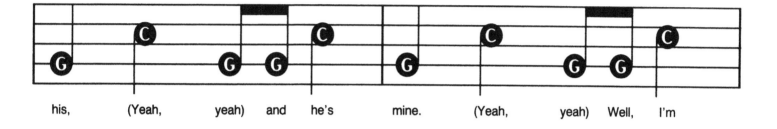

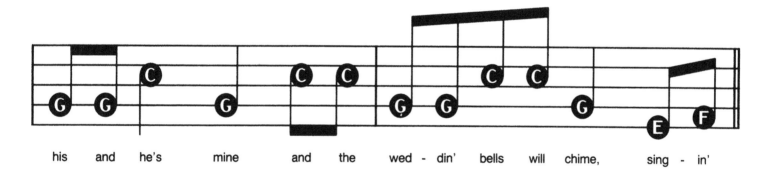

Repeat and Fade

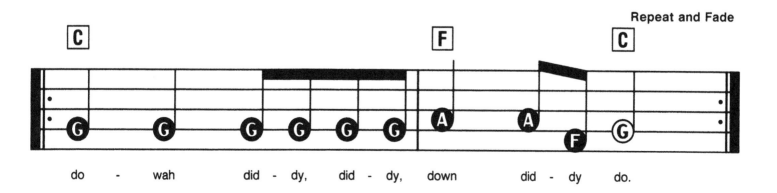

Donna

Registration 8
Rhythm: Slow Rock or 12 Beat

Words and Music by
Ritchie Valens

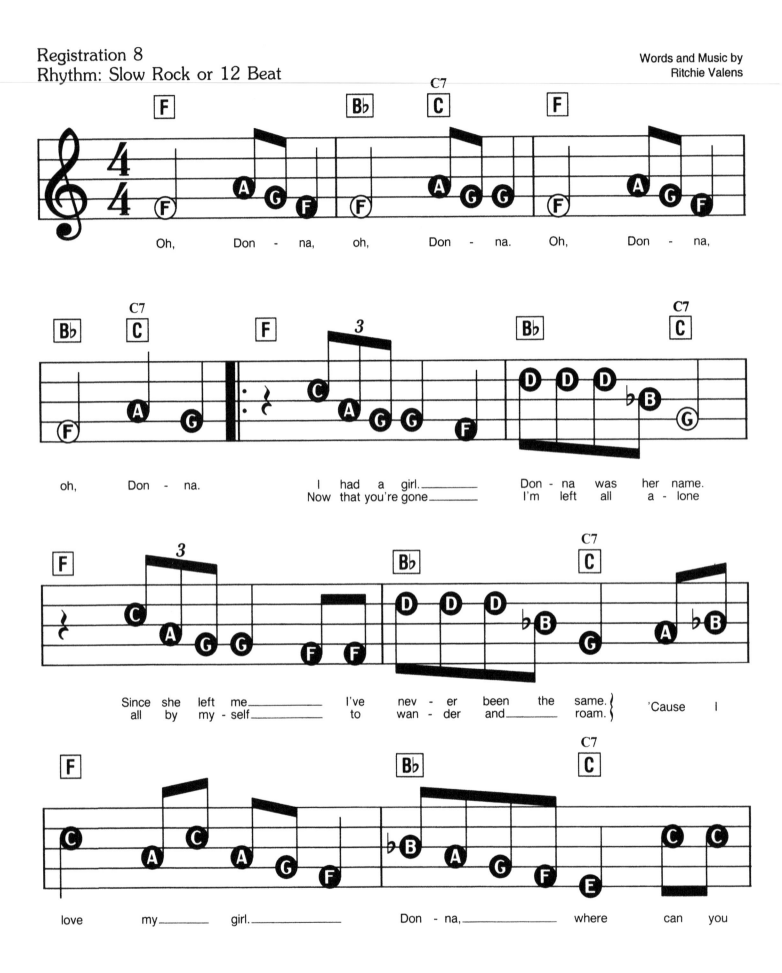

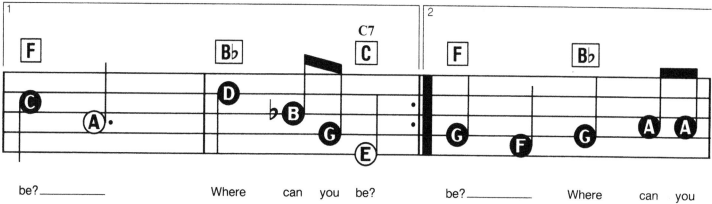

be?_____ Where can you be?   be?_____ Where can you

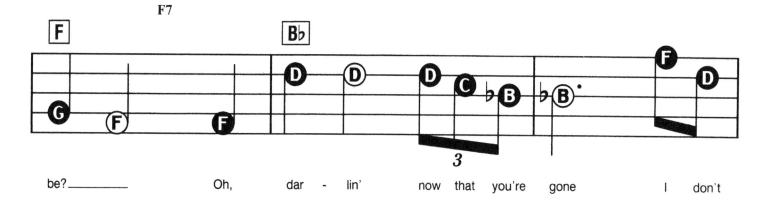

be?_____ Oh, dar - lin' now that you're gone I don't

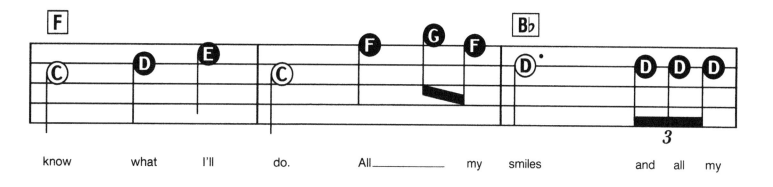

know what I'll do. All_____ my smiles and all my

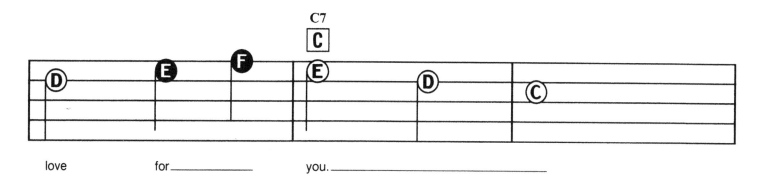

love for_____ you._____

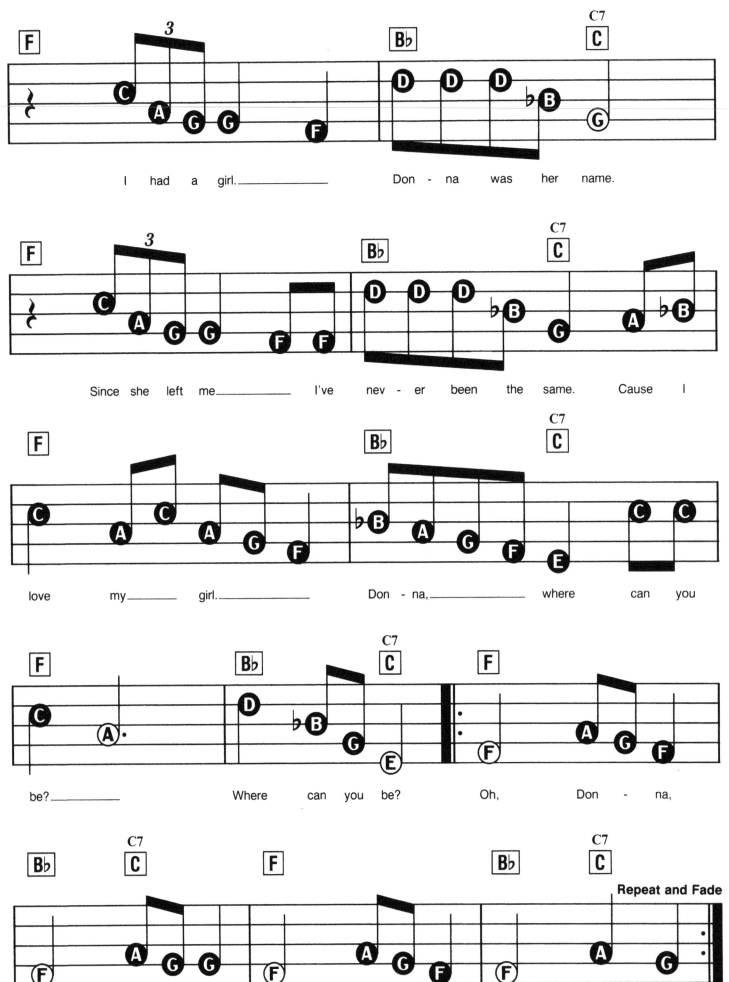

Great Balls of Fire

Registration 5
Rhythm: Rock or Jazz Rock

Words and Music by Otis Blackwell
and Jack Hammer

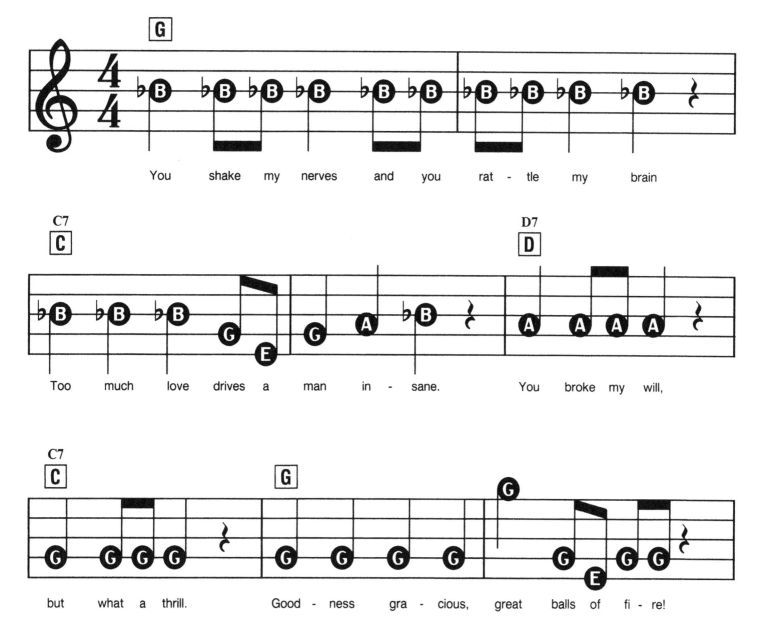

You shake my nerves and you rat - tle my brain

Too much love drives a man in - sane. You broke my will,

but what a thrill. Good - ness gra - cious, great balls of fi - re!

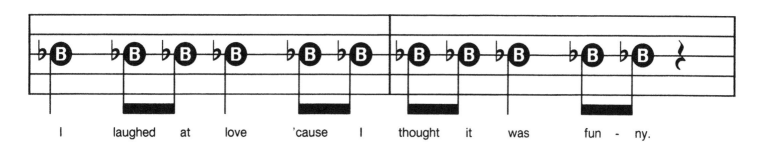

I laughed at love 'cause I thought it was fun - ny.

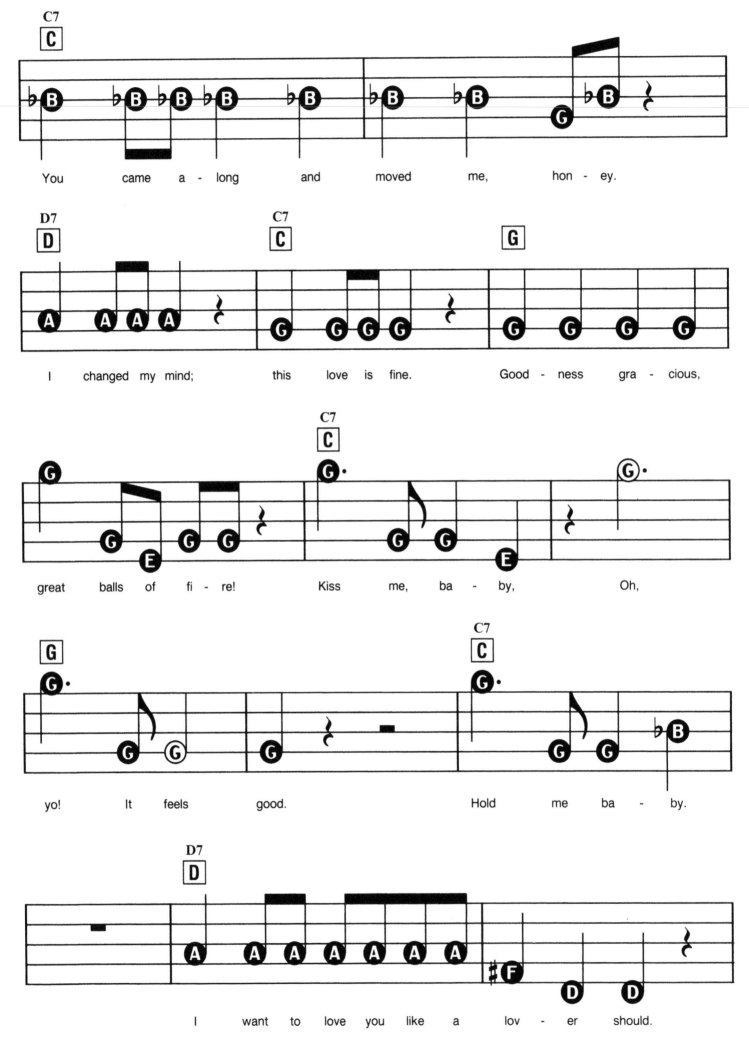

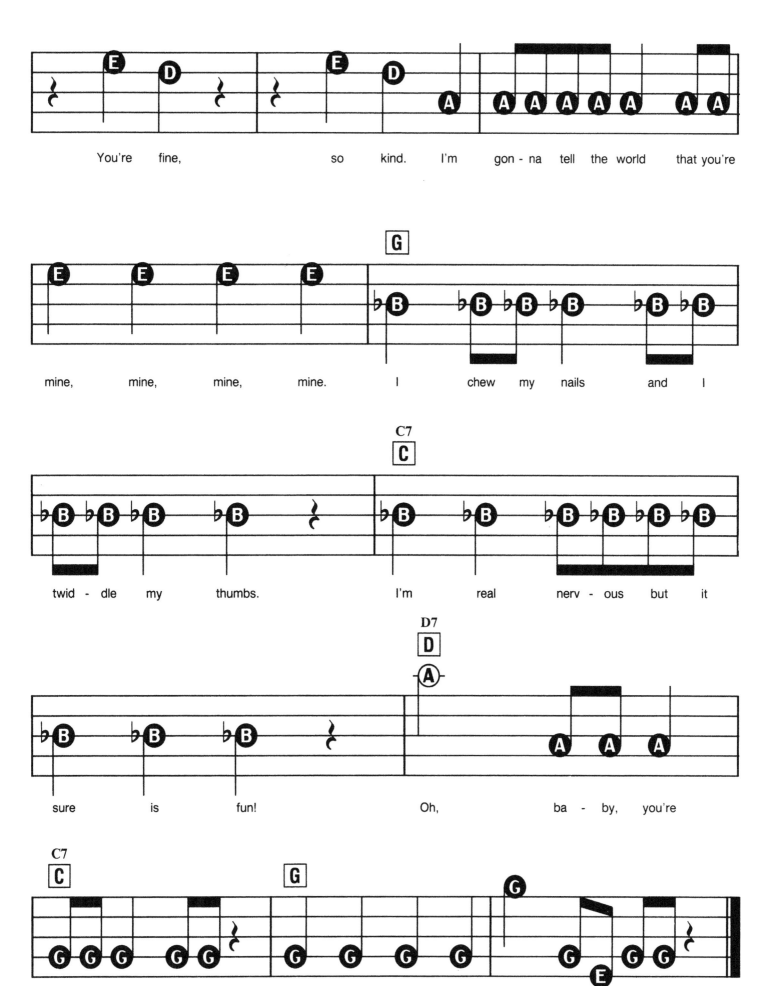

Hang On Sloopy

Registration 2
Rhythm: Rock

Words and Music by Wes Farrell
and Bert Russell

Hang on Sloo - py, Sloo-py hang on.

Sloo - py lives in a ver - y bad part of
Sloo - py, I don't _____ care what your _____ dad - dy
Sloo - py, let your hair down, ____ let it down _____ on

town.
do.   All the girls I know, they try to
me.   Don't you know, lit - tle girl, ____ I'm ____
           Come on Sloo - py, let your hair down, __

1, 2

put my Sloo - py down.
in _____ love with you?
girl, let it down on me.

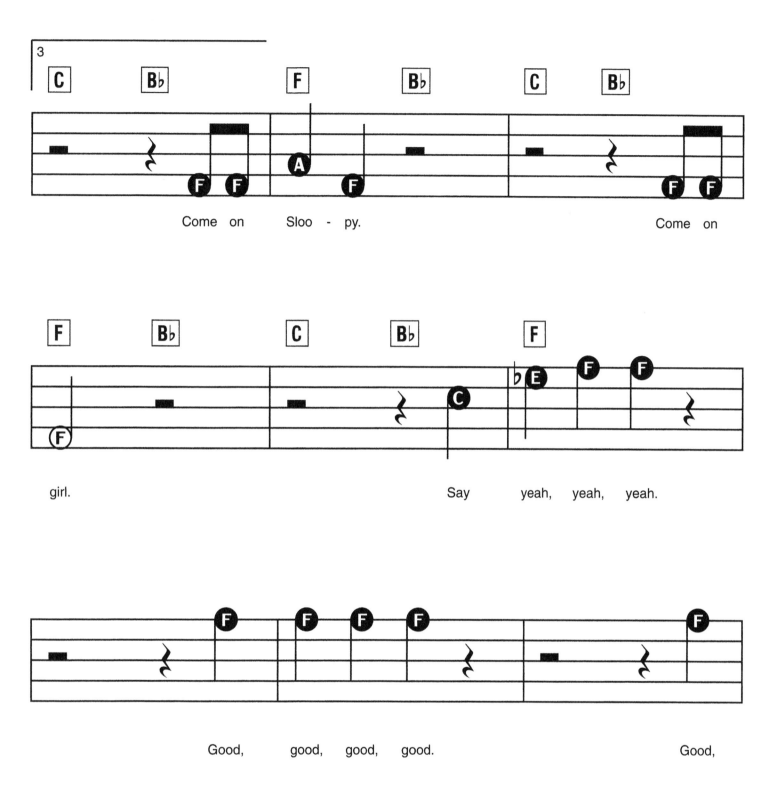

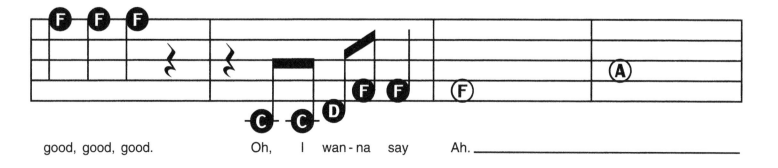

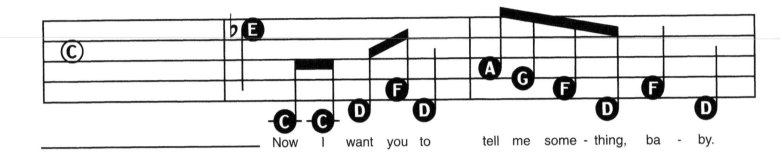

Now I want you to tell me some - thing, ba - by.

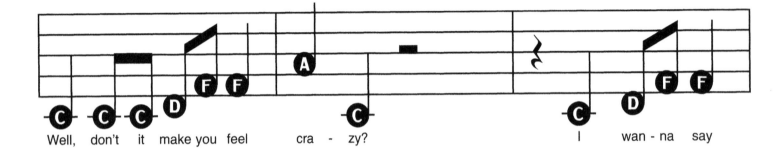

Well, don't it make you feel cra - zy? I wan - na say

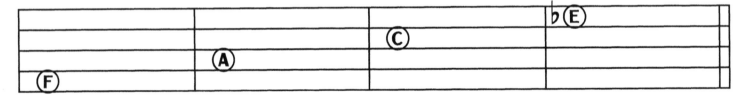

Ah.

Repeat and Fade

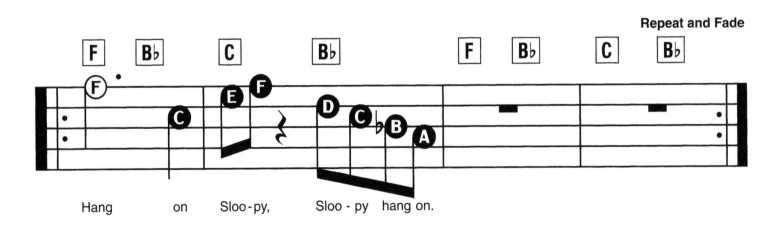

Hang on Sloo - py, Sloo - py hang on.

Hound Dog

Registration 4
Rhythm: Rock 'n' Roll or Swing

Words and Music by Jerry Leiber
and Mike Stoller

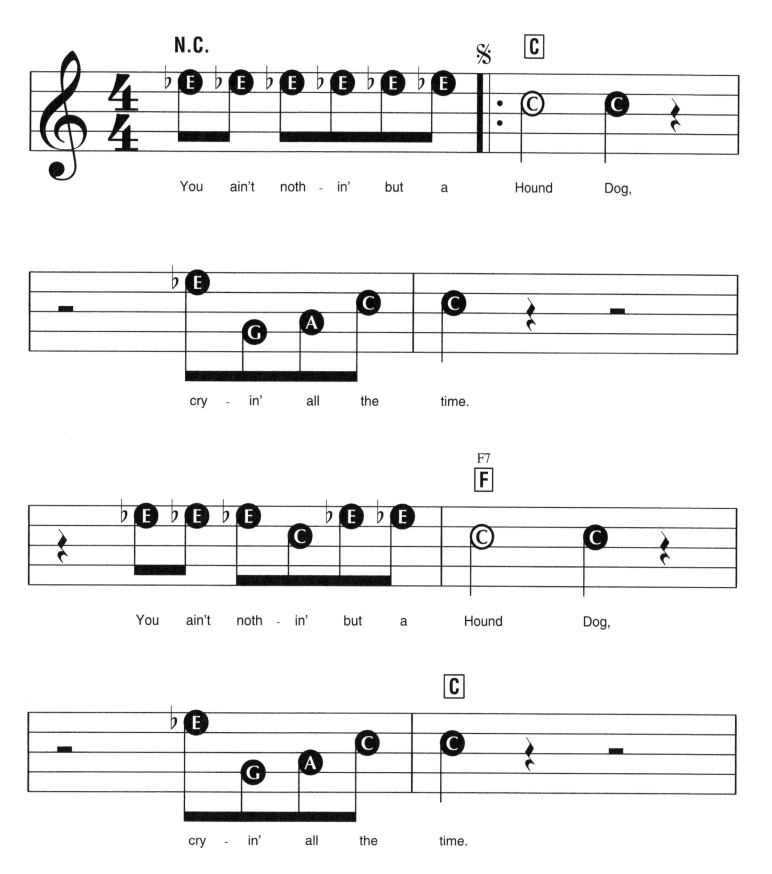

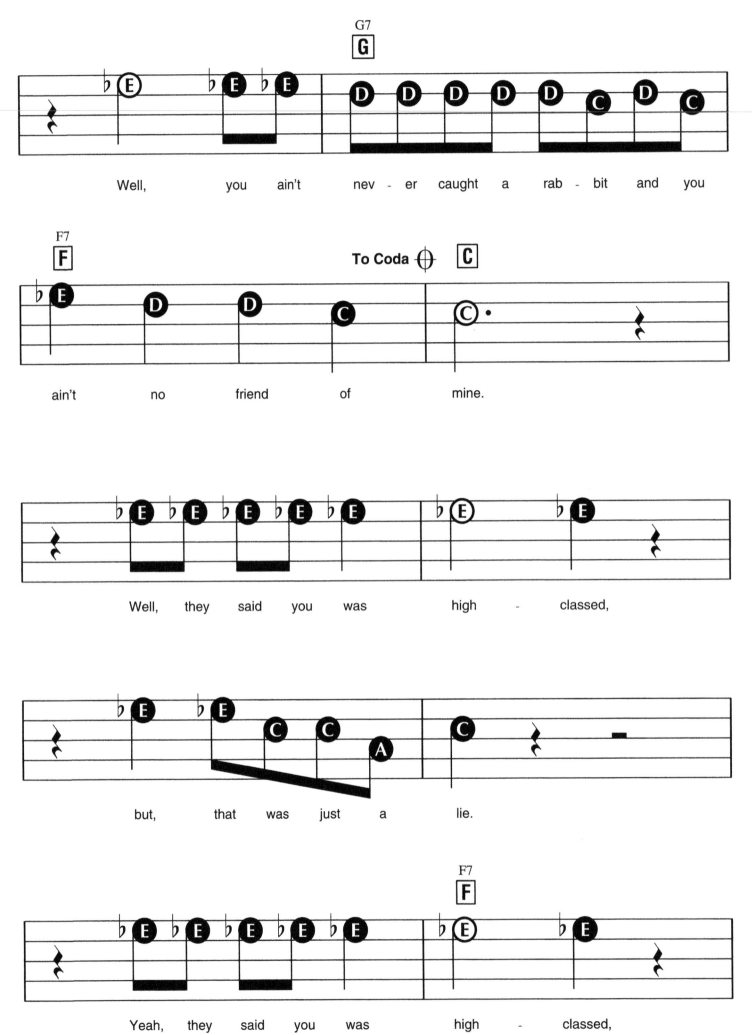

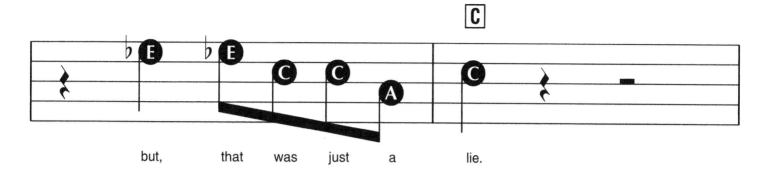

but, that was just a lie.

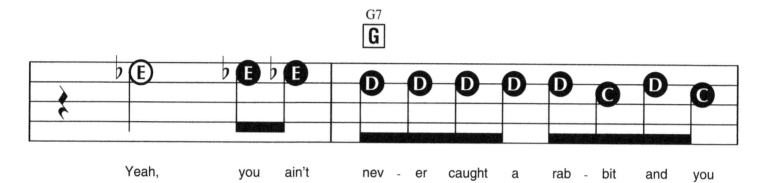

Yeah, you ain't nev - er caught a rab - bit and you

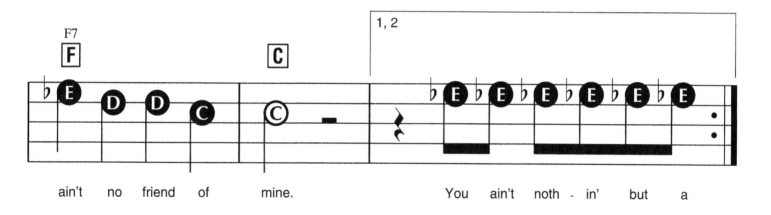

ain't no friend of mine. You ain't noth - in' but a

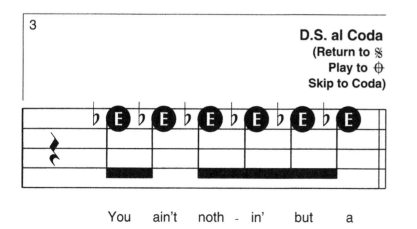

D.S. al Coda
(Return to %
Play to ⊕
Skip to Coda)

You ain't noth - in' but a

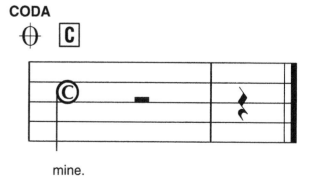

CODA

mine.

Kansas City

Registration 4
Rhythm: Shuffle or Swing

Words and Music by Jerry Leiber
and Mike Stoller

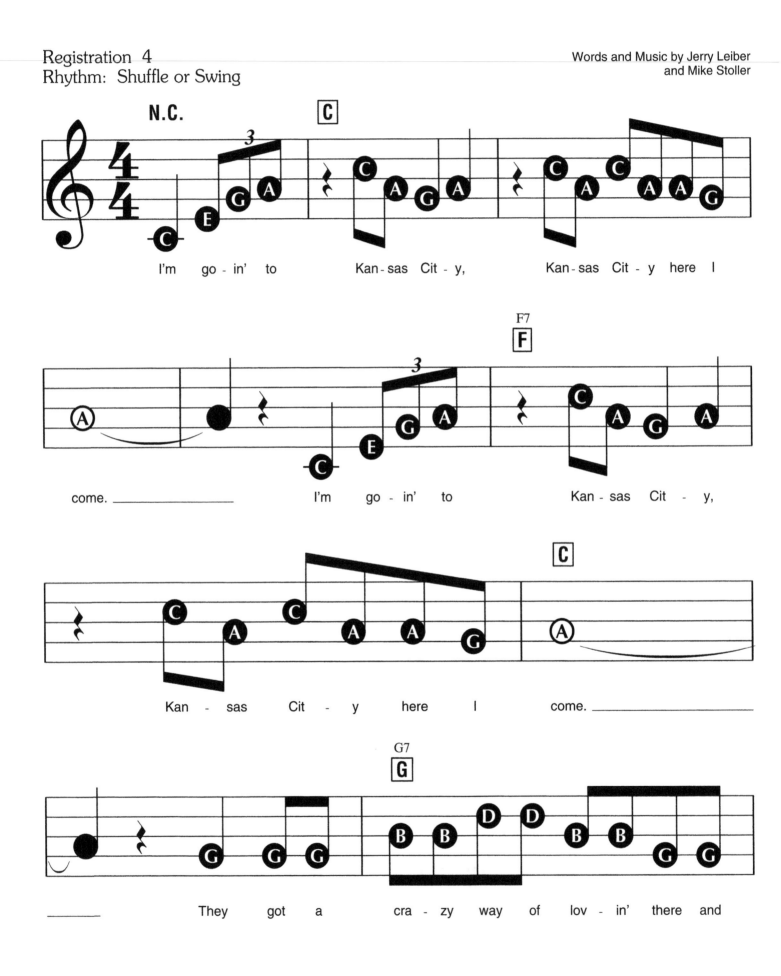

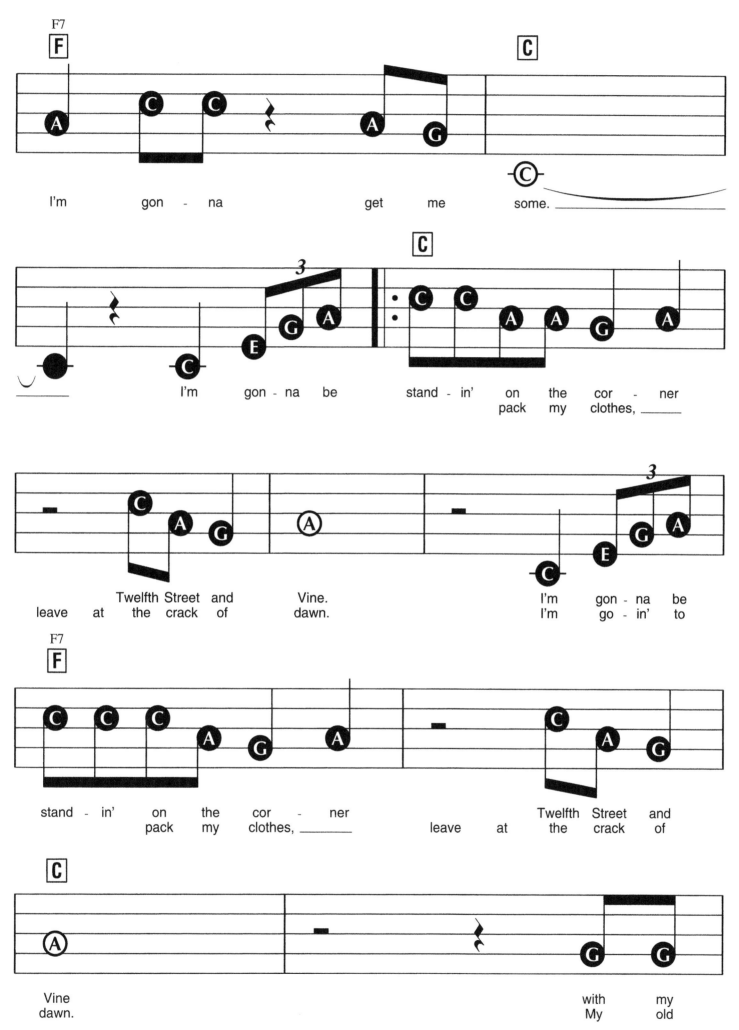

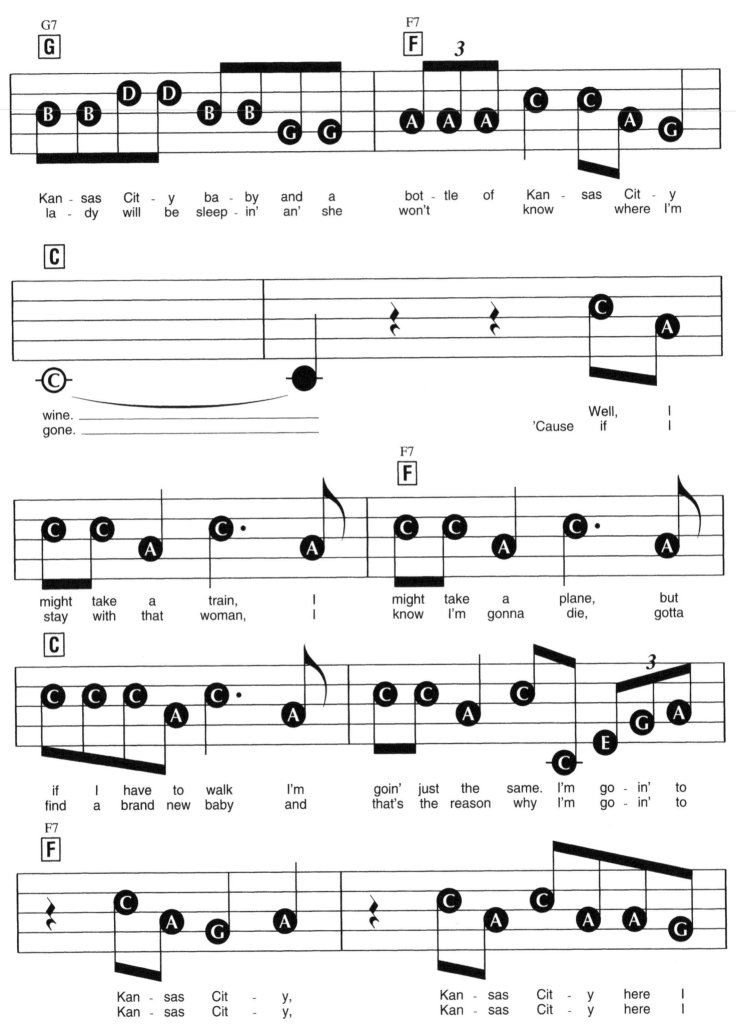

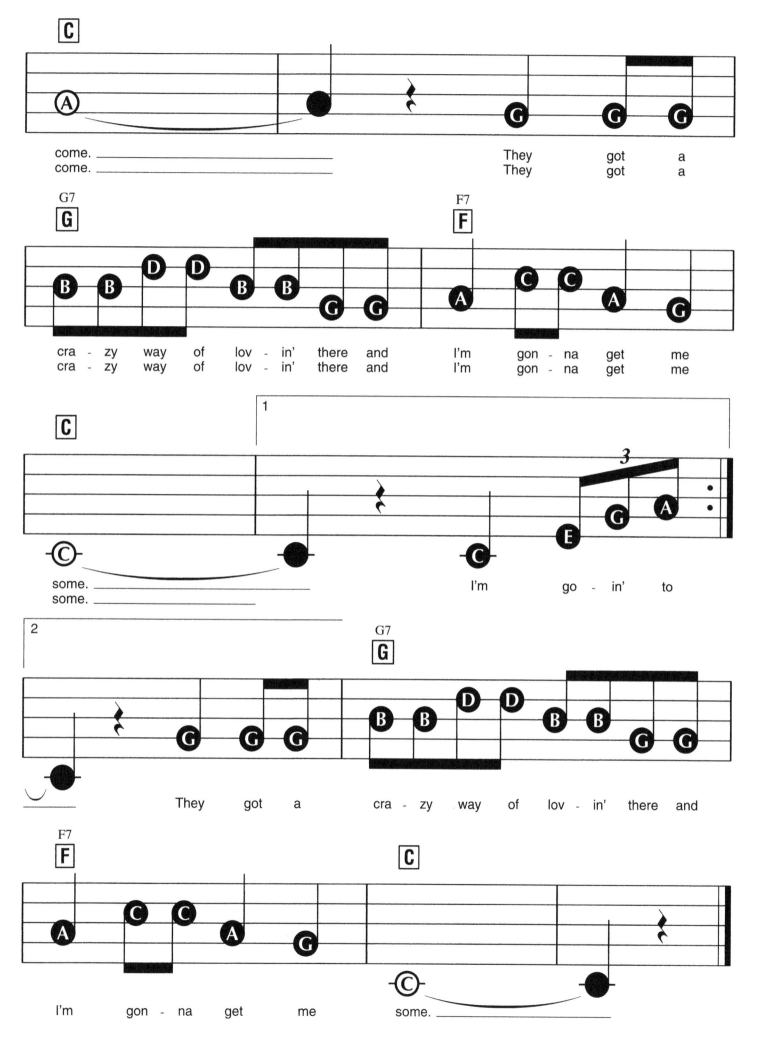

Love Me Do

Registration 6
Rhythm: Country Swing

Words and Music by John Lennon
and Paul McCartney

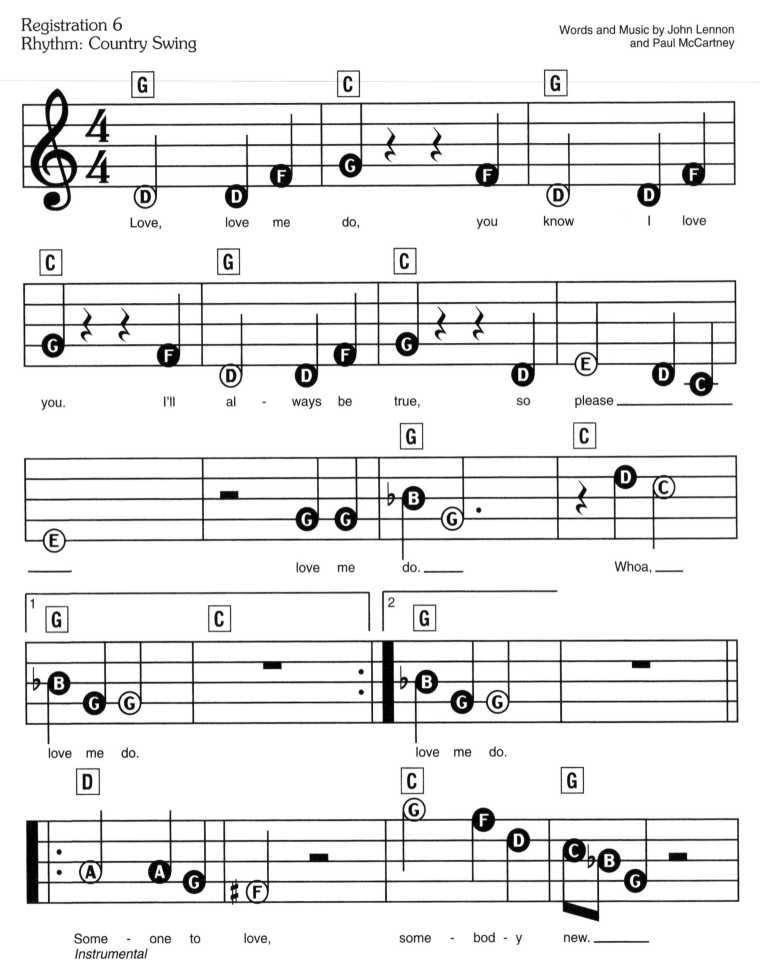

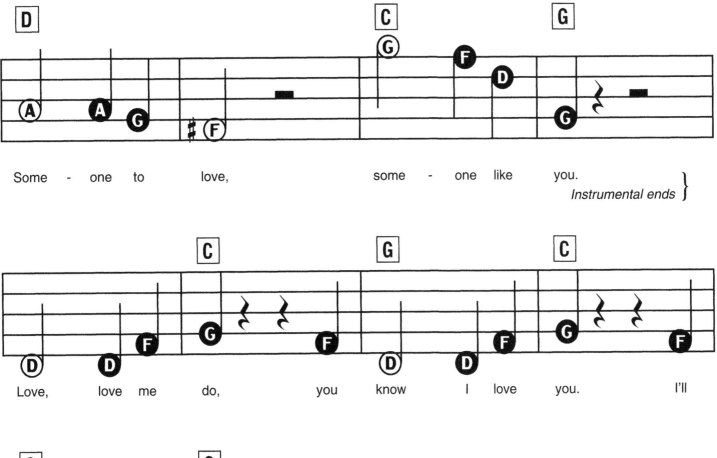

Some - one to love, some - one like you.
Instrumental ends }

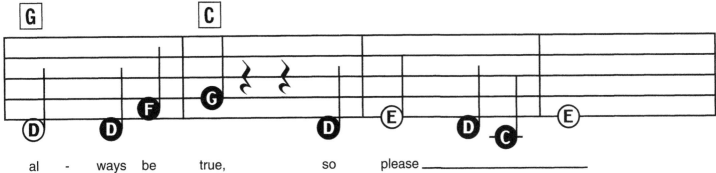

Love, love me do, you know I love you. I'll

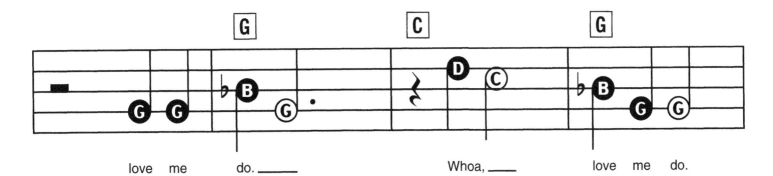

al - ways be true, so please _____

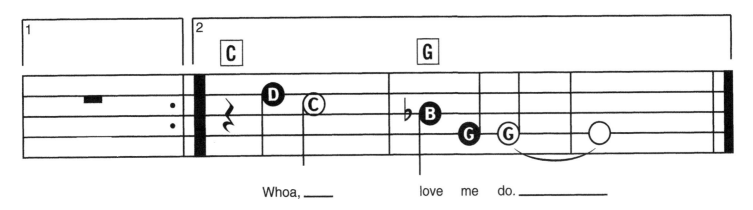

love me do. _____ Whoa, _____ love me do.

Whoa, _____ love me do. _____

Mellow Yellow

Registration 1
Rhythm: 8 Beat or Rock

Words and Music by
Donovan Leitch

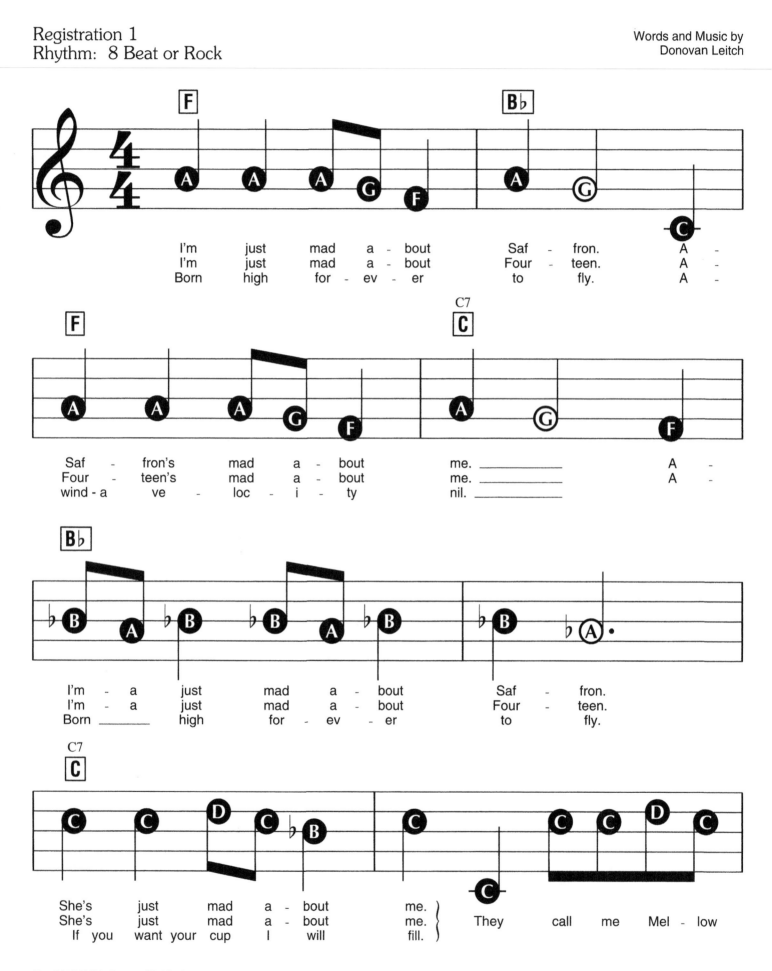

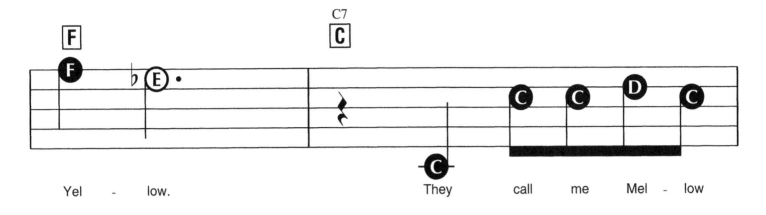

Yel - low.   They call me Mel - low

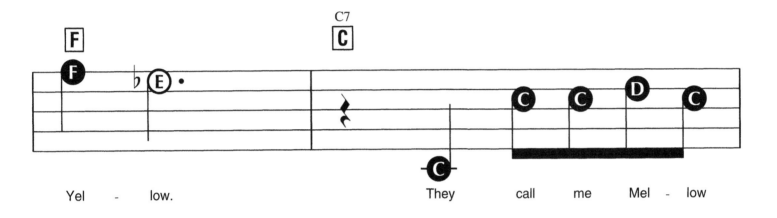

Yel - low.   They call me Mel - low

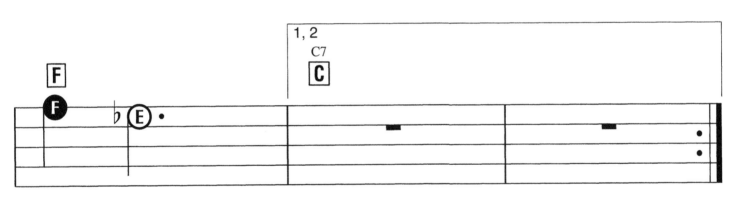

Yel - low.

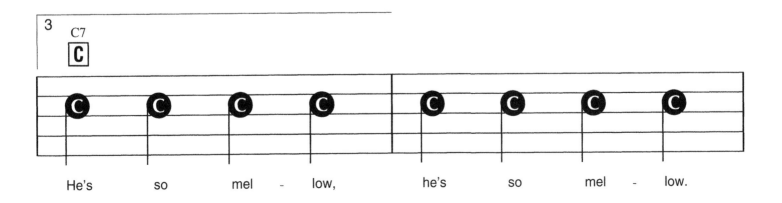

He's   so   mel - low,   he's   so   mel - low.

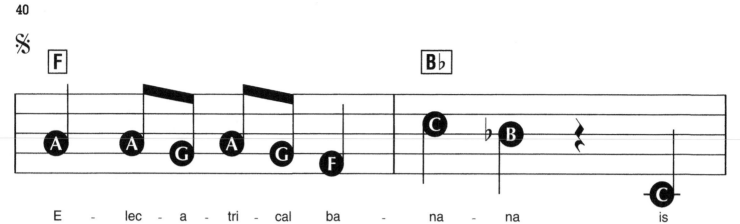

E - lec - a - tri - cal ba - na - na is

Instrumental

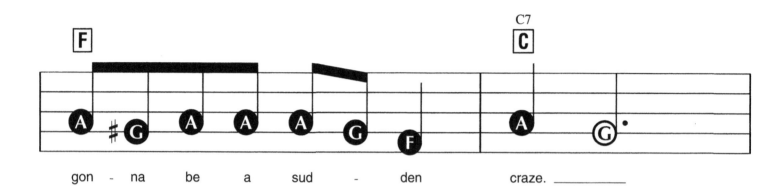

gon - na be a sud - den craze. _____

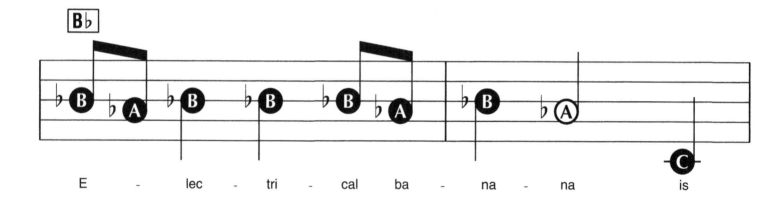

E - lec - tri - cal ba - na - na is

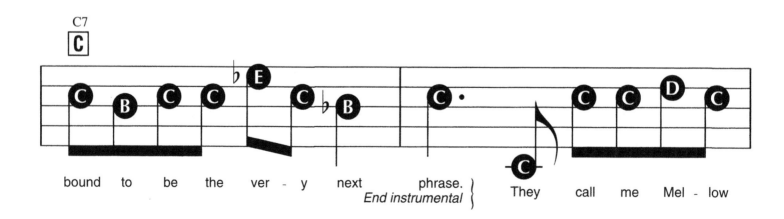

bound to be the ver - y next phrase. }

End instrumental

They call me Mel - low

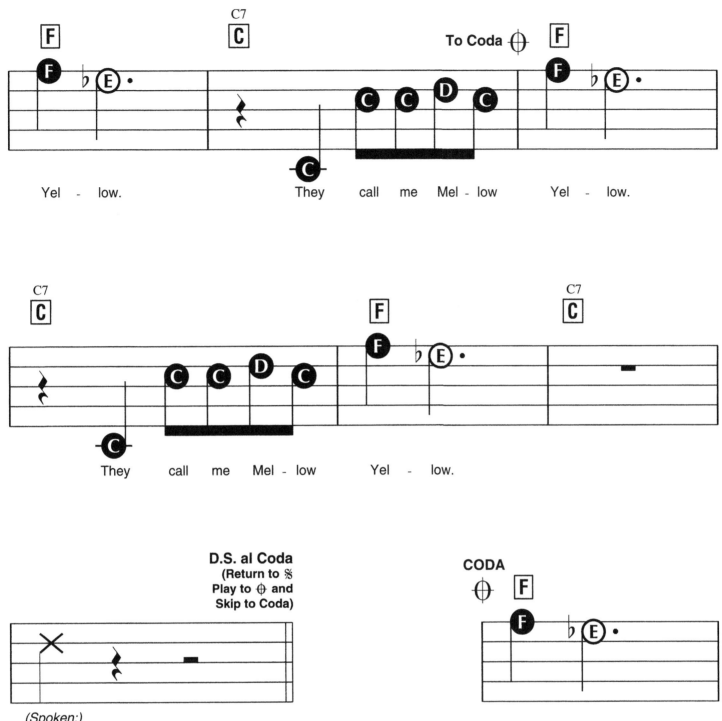

Yel - low.   They call me Mel - low   Yel - low.

They call me Mel - low   Yel - low.

D.S. al Coda
(Return to %
Play to ⊕ and
Skip to Coda)

(Spoken:)
Yeah!

CODA

Yel - low.

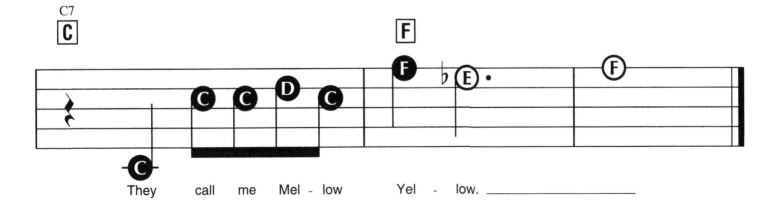

They call me Mel - low   Yel - low. _____

Mony, Mony

Registration 8
Rhythm: Rock

Words and Music by Bobby Bloom, Tommy James,
Ritchie Cordell and Bo Gentry

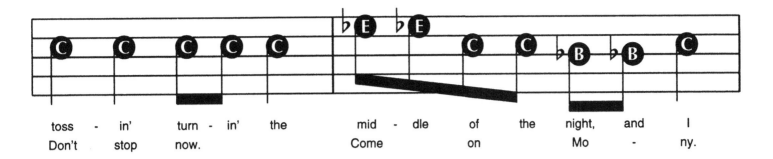

toss - in' turn - in' the mid - dle of the night, and I
Don't stop now. Come on Mo - ny.

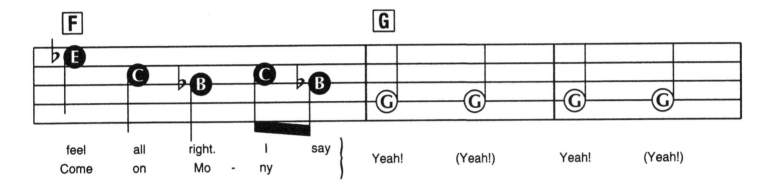

feel all right. I say Yeah! (Yeah!) Yeah! (Yeah!)
Come on Mo - ny

Yeah! (Yeah!) Yeah! (Yeah!) Yeah! (Yeah!) Yeah! You make me feel. (Mo - ny, Mo - ny)

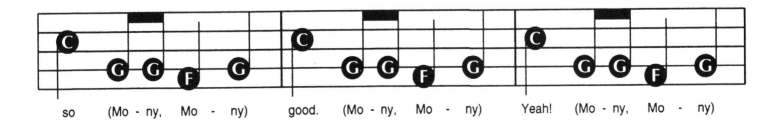

so (Mo - ny, Mo - ny) good. (Mo - ny, Mo - ny) Yeah! (Mo - ny, Mo - ny)

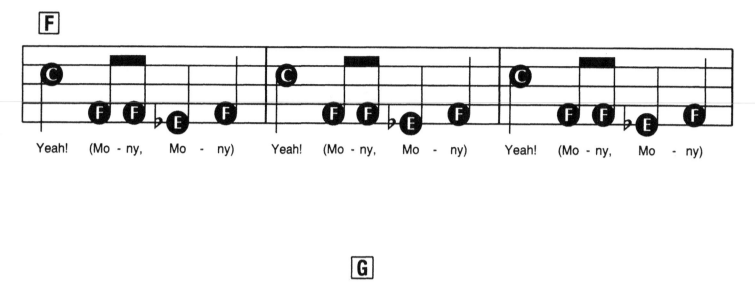

Yeah! (Mo - ny, Mo - ny) Yeah! (Mo - ny, Mo - ny) Yeah! (Mo - ny, Mo - ny)

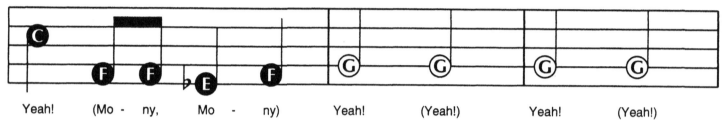

Yeah! (Mo - ny, Mo - ny) Yeah! (Yeah!) Yeah! (Yeah!)

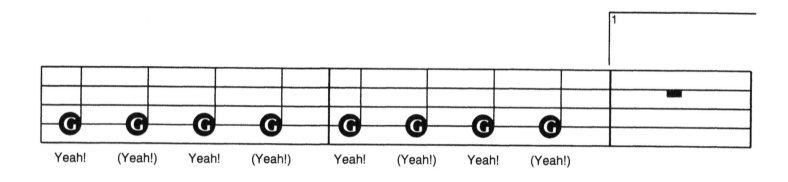

Yeah! (Yeah!) Yeah! (Yeah!) Yeah! (Yeah!) Yeah! (Yeah!)

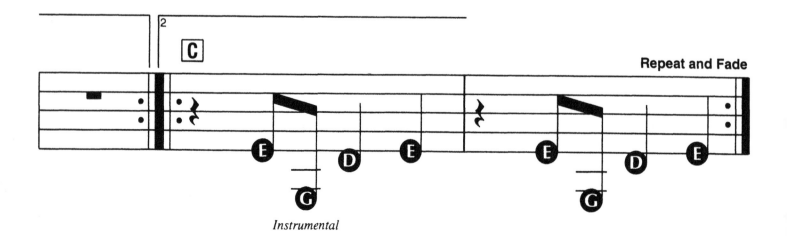

Repeat and Fade

Instrumental

Rockin' Robin

Registration 5
Rhythm: Shuffle or Swing

Words and Music by
J. Thomas

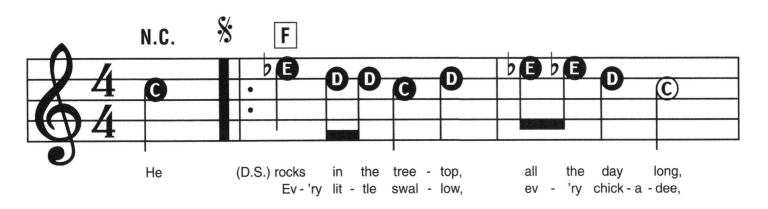

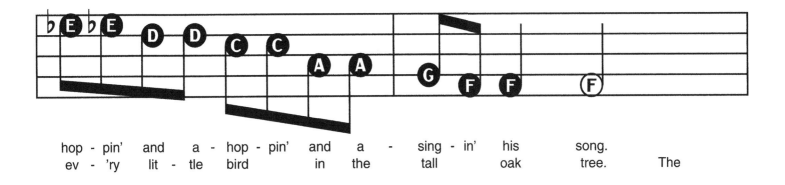

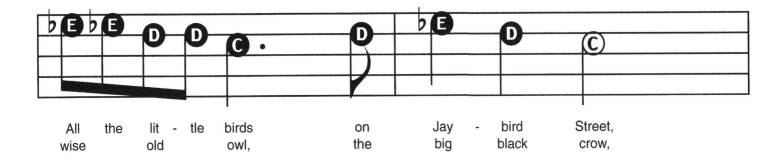

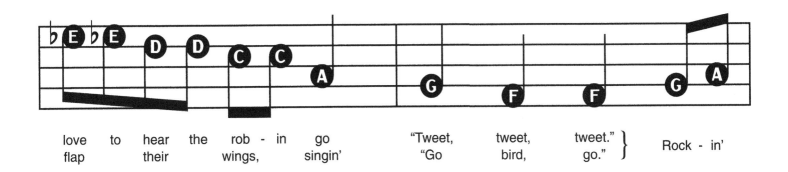

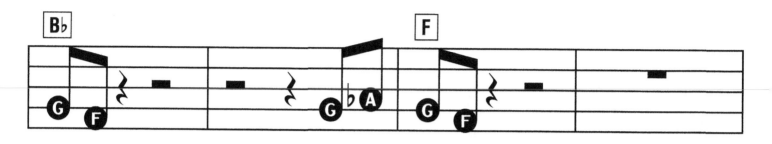

Rob - in,   Rock - in'   Rob - in,

To Coda

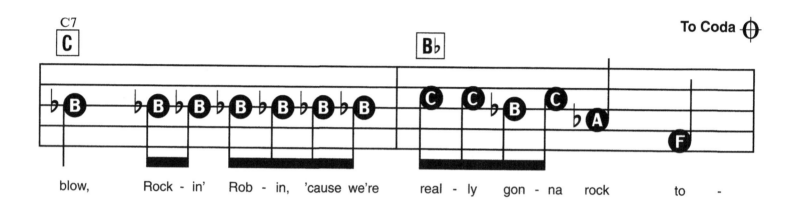

blow,   Rock - in'   Rob - in, 'cause we're   real - ly   gon - na   rock   to -

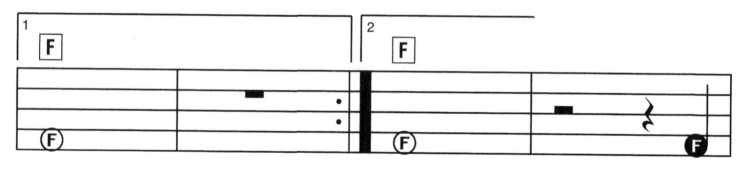

night.   night.   A

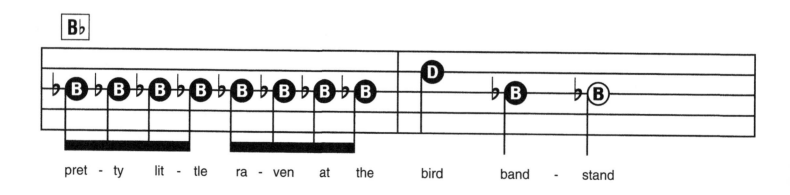

pret - ty   lit - tle   ra - ven   at   the   bird   band - stand

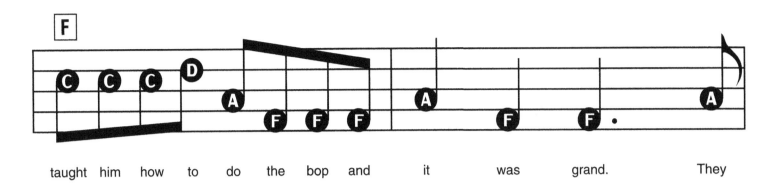

taught him how to do the bop and it was grand. They

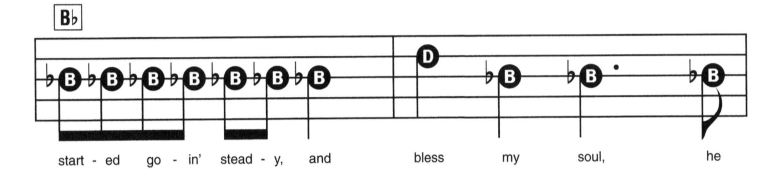

start - ed go - in' stead - y, and bless my soul, he

D.S. al Coda
(Return to 𝄋
Play to ⨁ and
Skip to Coda)

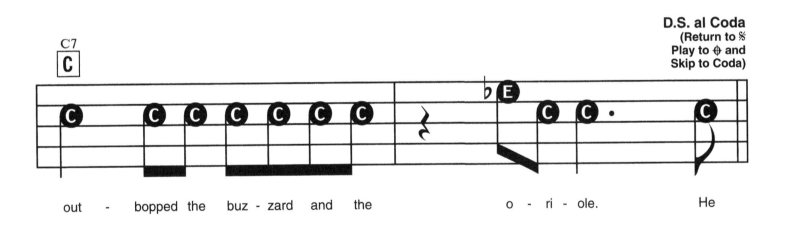

out - bopped the buz - zard and the o - ri - ole. He

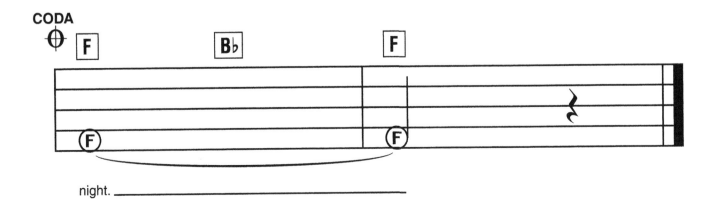

night. _____

No Particular Place to Go

Registration 3
Rhythm: Shuffle or Swing

Words and Music by
Chuck Berry

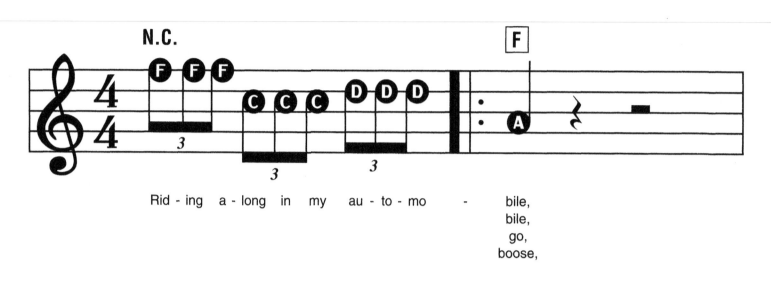

Rid - ing a - long in my au - to - mo - bile,
bile,
go,
boose,

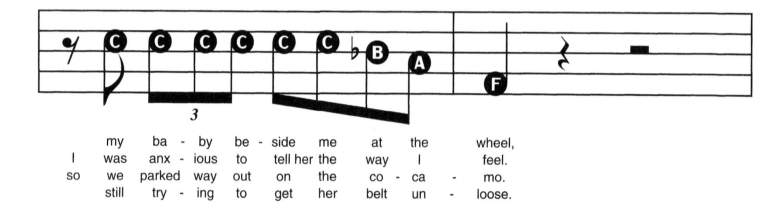

	my	ba - by	be - side	me	at	the	wheel,
I	was	anx - ious	to	tell her	the	way	I	feel.
so	we	parked	way	out	on	the	co - ca -	mo.
still	try - ing	to	get	her	belt	un -	loose.

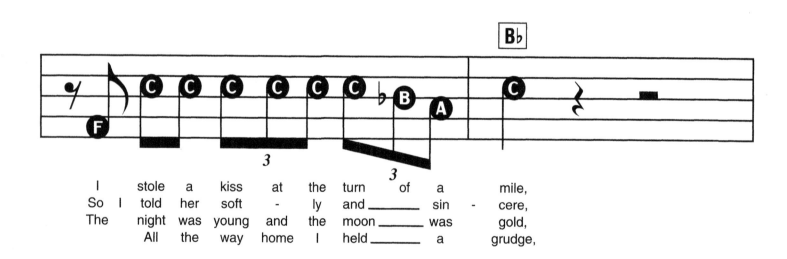

I	stole	a	kiss	at	the	turn	of	a	mile,
So I	told	her	soft -	ly	and ____	sin -	cere,
The	night	was	young	and	the	moon ____	was	gold,
All	the	way	home	I	held ____	a	grudge,

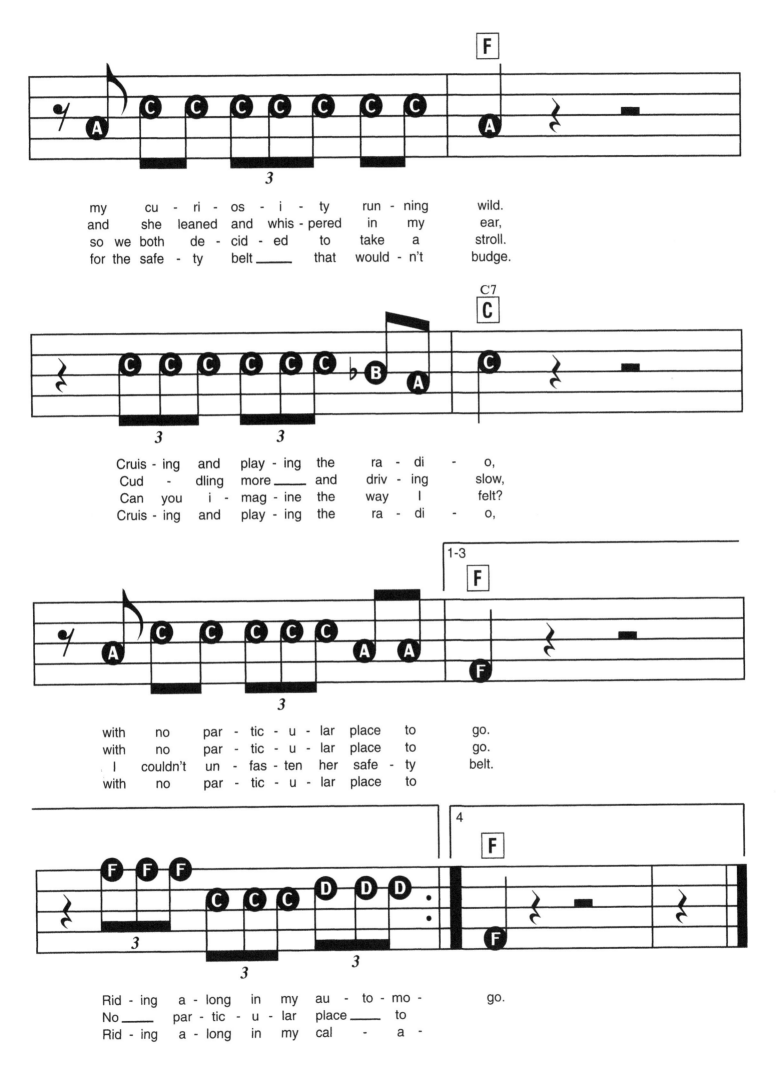

my   cu - ri - os - i - ty   run - ning   wild.
and   she   leaned   and   whis - pered   in   my   ear,
so   we   both   de - cid - ed   to   take   a   stroll.
for   the   safe - ty   belt _____   that   would - n't   budge.

Cruis - ing   and   play - ing   the   ra - di - o,
Cud - dling   more _____   and   driv - ing   slow,
Can   you   i - mag - ine   the   way   I   felt?
Cruis - ing   and   play - ing   the   ra - di - o,

with   no   par - tic - u - lar   place   to   go.
with   no   par - tic - u - lar   place   to   go.
I   couldn't   un - fas - ten   her   safe - ty   belt.
with   no   par - tic - u - lar   place   to

Rid - ing   a - long   in   my   au - to - mo -   go.
No _____   par - tic - u - lar   place _____   to
Rid - ing   a - long   in   my   cal - a -

Rock Around the Clock

Registration 8
Rhythm: Rock 'n' Roll

Words and Music by Max C. Freedman
and Jimmy DeKnight

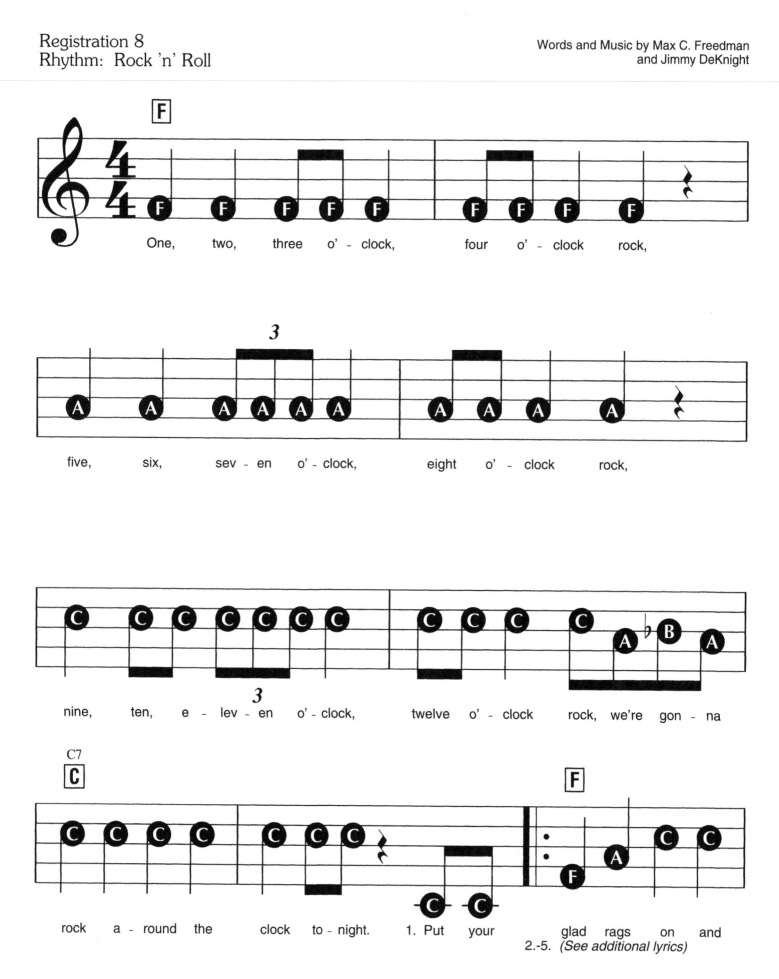

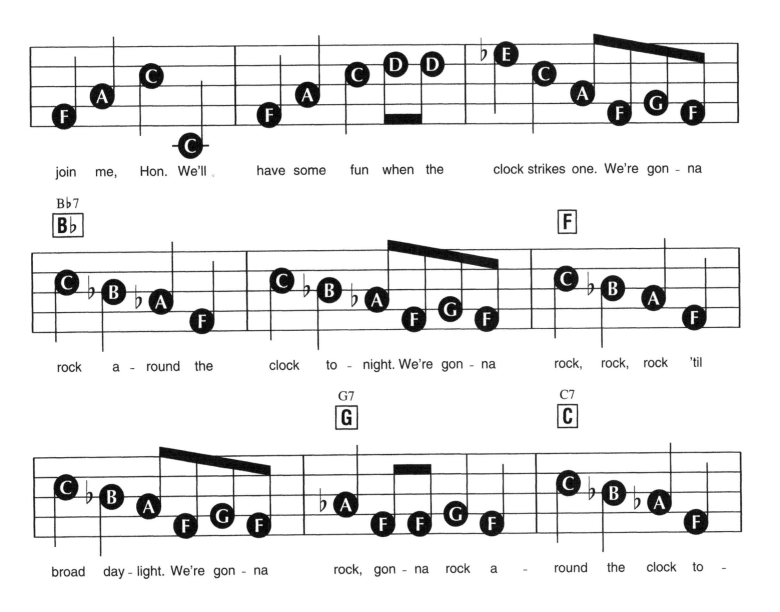

join me, Hon. We'll have some fun when the clock strikes one. We're gon - na

rock a - round the clock to - night. We're gon - na rock, rock, rock 'til

broad day - light. We're gon - na rock, gon - na rock a - round the clock to -

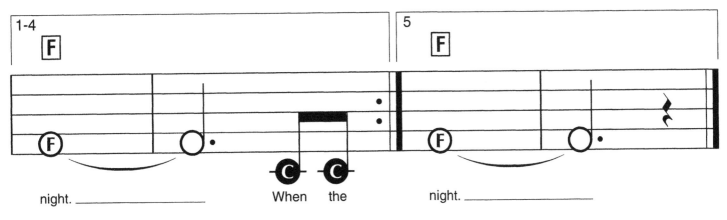

night. _____ When the night. _____

Additional Lyrics

2. When the clock strikes two, and three and four,
   If the band slows down we'll yell for more,
   We're gonna rock around the clock tonight,
   We're gonna rock, rock, rock, etc....

3. When the chimes ring five and six and seven,
   We'll be rockin' up in seventh heav'n.
   We're gonna rock around the clock tonight,
   We're gonna rock, rock, rock, etc....

4. When it's eight, nine, ten, eleven, too,
   I'll be goin' strong and so will you,
   We're gonna rock around the clock tonight,
   We're gonna rock, rock, rock, etc....

5. When the clock strikes twelve, we'll cool off, then,
   Start a rockin' 'round the clock again,
   We're gonna rock around the clock tonight,
   We're gonna rock, rock, rock, etc....

Save the Last Dance for Me

Registration 3
Rhythm: Ballad or Fox Trot

Words and Music by Doc Pomus
and Mort Shuman

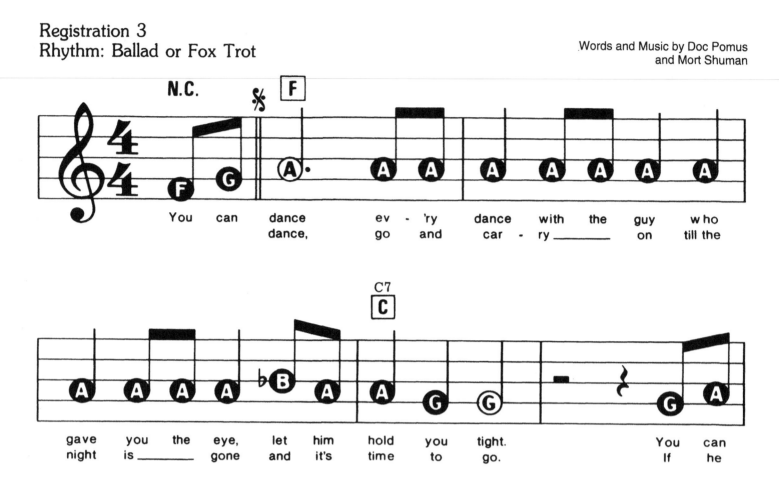

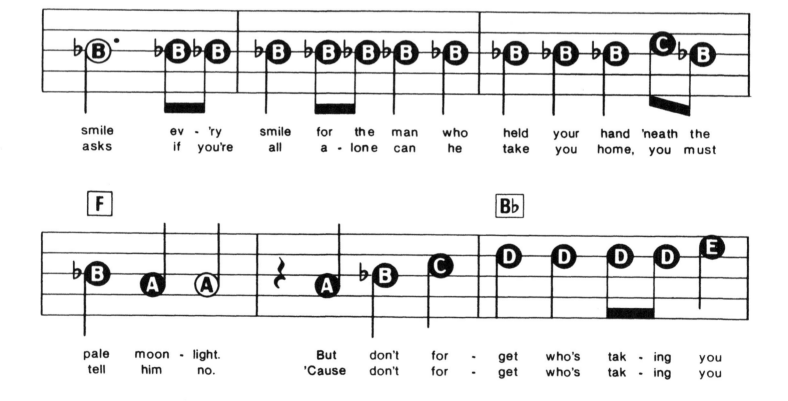

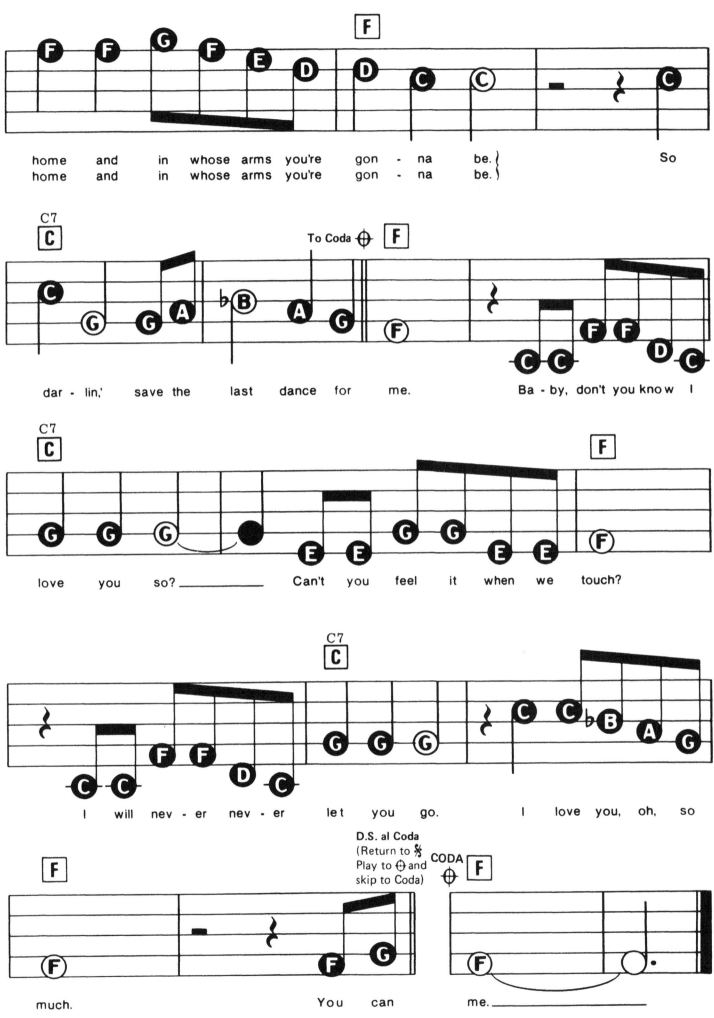

See You Later, Alligator

Registration 2
Rhythm: Shuffle or Swing

Words and Music by
Robert Guidry

N.C.

Well, I saw my ba - by walk - ing
told me,
dad - dy,
'ga - tor,

with an - oth - er man to - day. _____
near - ly made me lose my head. _____
you know my love is just for you. _____
I know you meant it just for play. _____

F7 / F

Well, I saw my ba - by walk - ing
When I thought of what she told me,
She said, I'm sor - ry, pret - ty dad - dy,
I said, wait a min - ute, 'ga - tor,

C

with an - oth - er man to - day. _____
near - ly made me lose my head. _____
you know my love is just for you. _____
I know you meant it just for play. _____

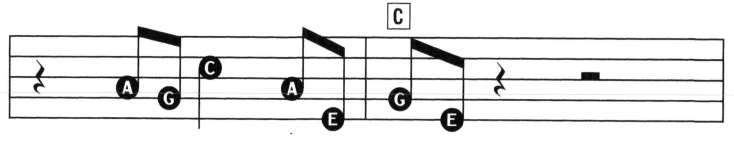

af - ter 'while, croc - o - dile. _____

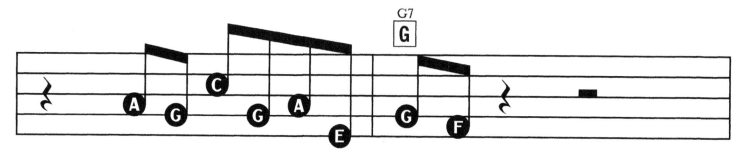

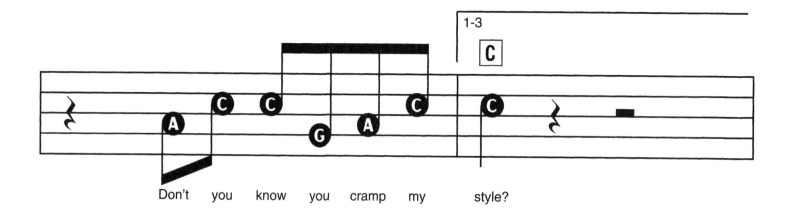

G7

Can't you see you're in my way now?

1-3

Don't you know you cramp my style?

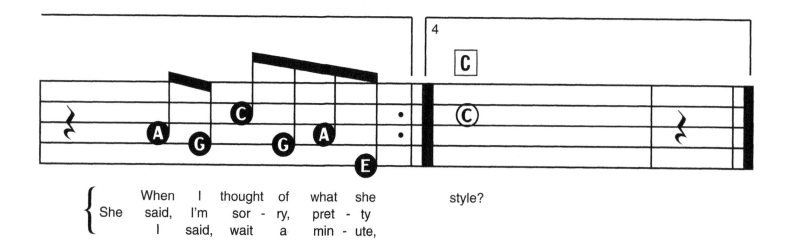

4

{ When I thought of what she style?
She said, I'm sor - ry, pret - ty
I said, wait a min - ute,

Twist and Shout

Registration 4
Rhythm: Rock

Words and Music by Bert Russell
and Phil Medley

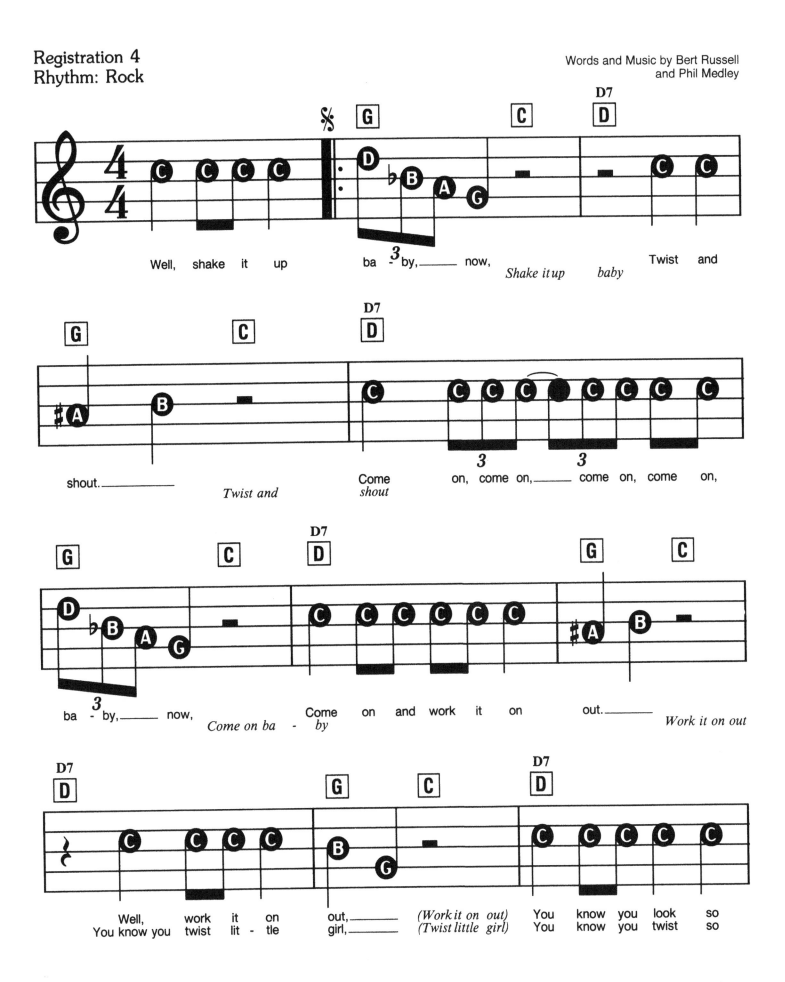

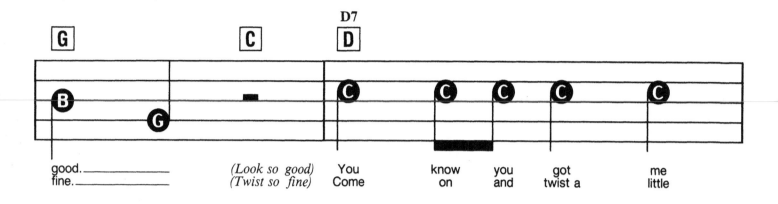

good. _____ (Look so good) You know you got me me
fine. _____ (Twist so fine) Come on and twist a little

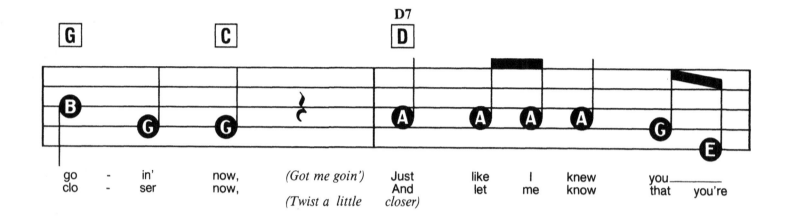

go - in' now, (Got me goin') Just like I knew you
clo - ser now, And let me know that you're
(Twist a little closer)

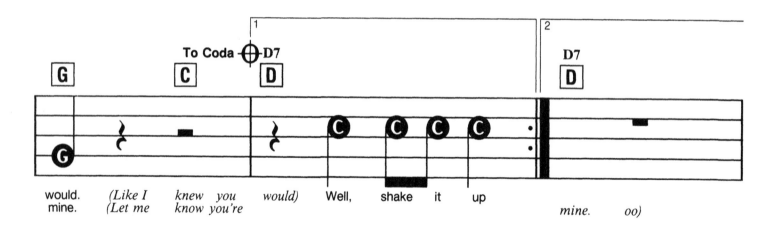

would. (Like I knew you would) Well, shake it up
mine. (Let me know you're mine. oo)

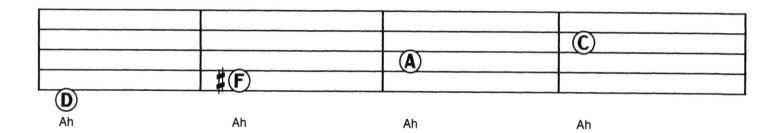

Ah   Ah   Ah   Ah

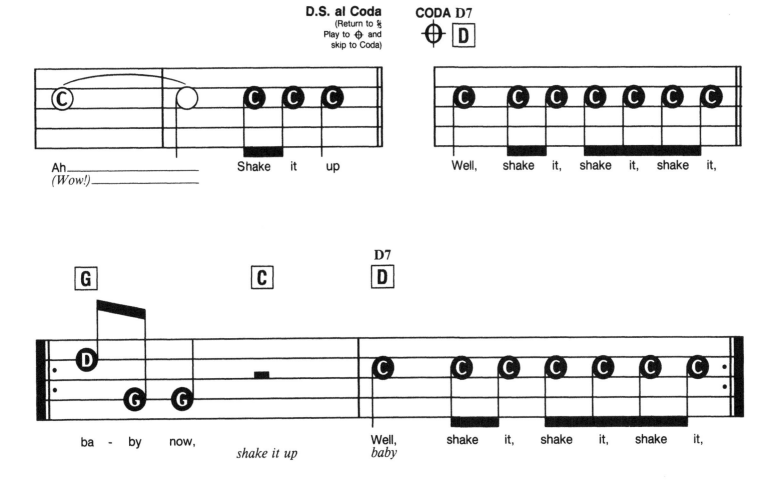

D.S. al Coda
(Return to %
Play to ⊕ and
skip to Coda)

CODA D7

Ah_____
*(Wow!)*_____

Shake it up

Well, shake it, shake it, shake it,

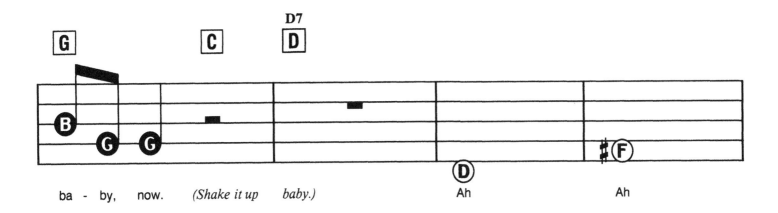

G   **C**   **D7 D**

ba - by now,   *shake it up*

Well, *baby*   shake it, shake it, shake it,

G   **C**   **D7 D**

ba - by, now. *(Shake it up baby.)*

Ah   Ah

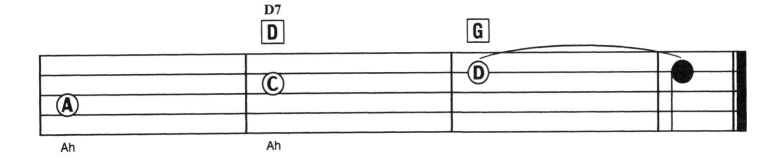

D7 D   **G**

Ah   Ah

Shake, Rattle and Roll

Registration 4
Rhythm: Rock or Fox Trot

Words and Music by
Charles Calhoun

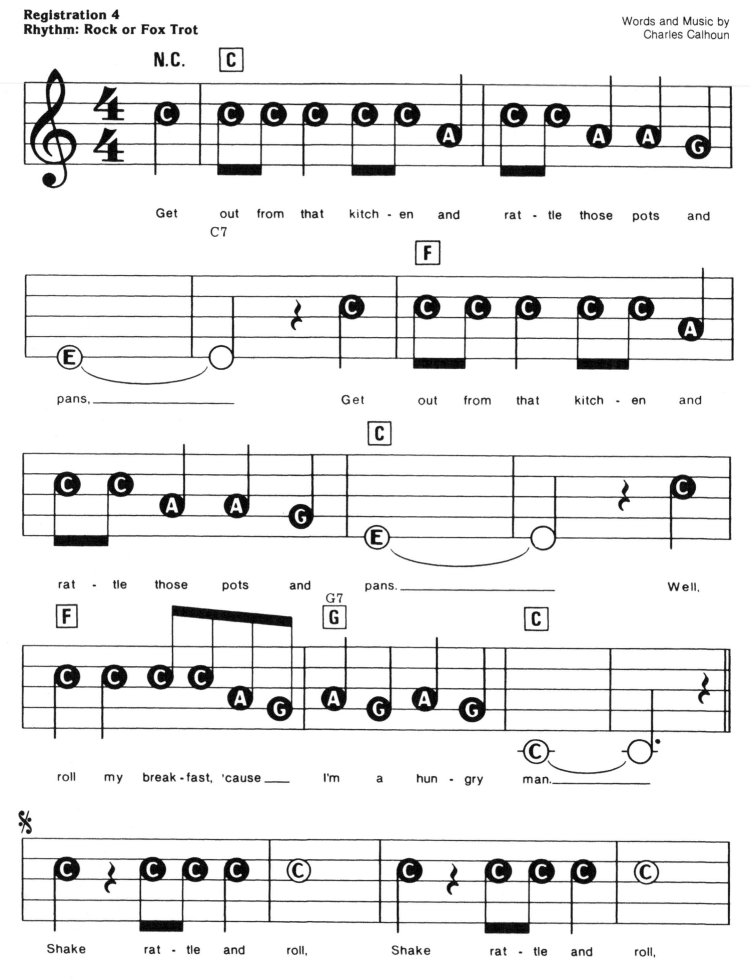

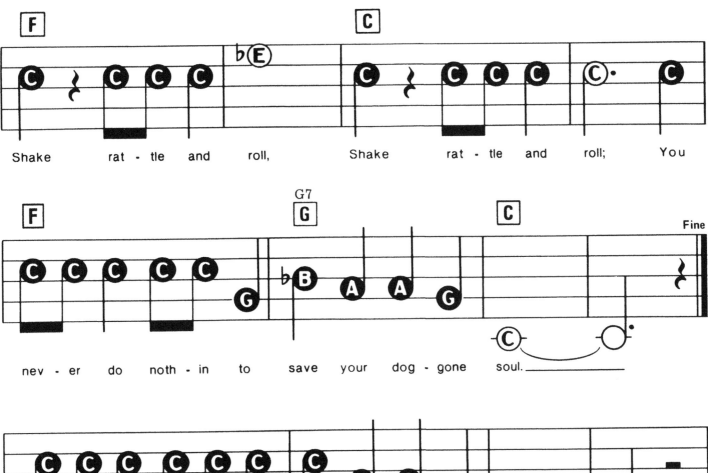

Shake rat - tle and roll, Shake rat - tle and roll; You

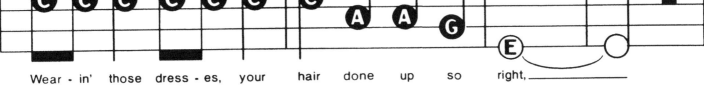

nev - er do noth - in to save your dog - gone soul. _____

Wear - in' those dress - es, your hair done up so right, _____

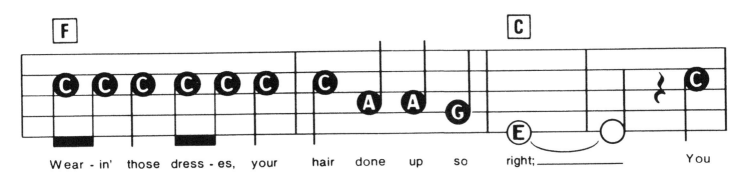

Wear - in' those dress - es, your hair done up so right; _____ You

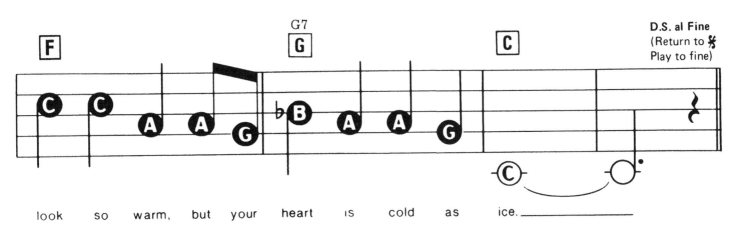

look so warm, but your heart is cold as ice. _____

Surfin' U.S.A.

Registration 4
Rhythm: Rock or Fox Trot

Words and Music by
Chuck Berry

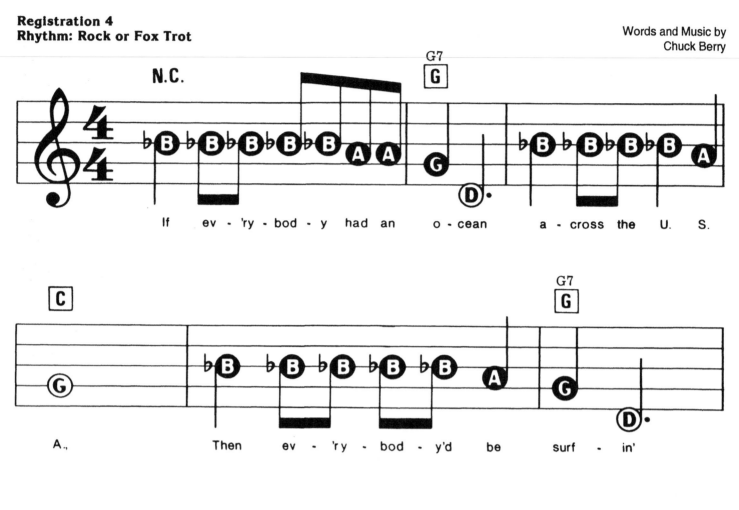

If ev - 'ry - bod - y had an o - cean a - cross the U. S.

A., Then ev - 'ry - bod - y'd be surf - in'

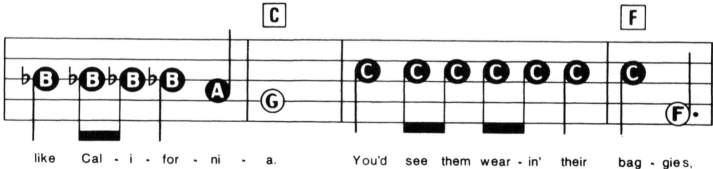

like Cal - i - for - ni - a. You'd see them wear - in' their bag - gies,

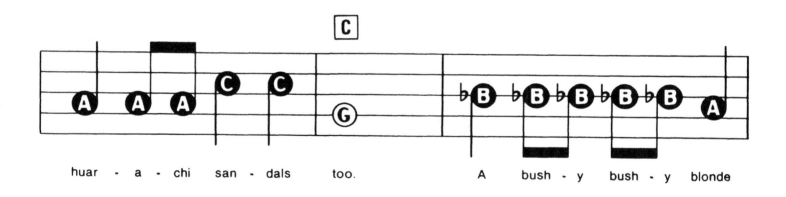

huar - a - chi san - dals too. A bush - y bush - y blonde

63

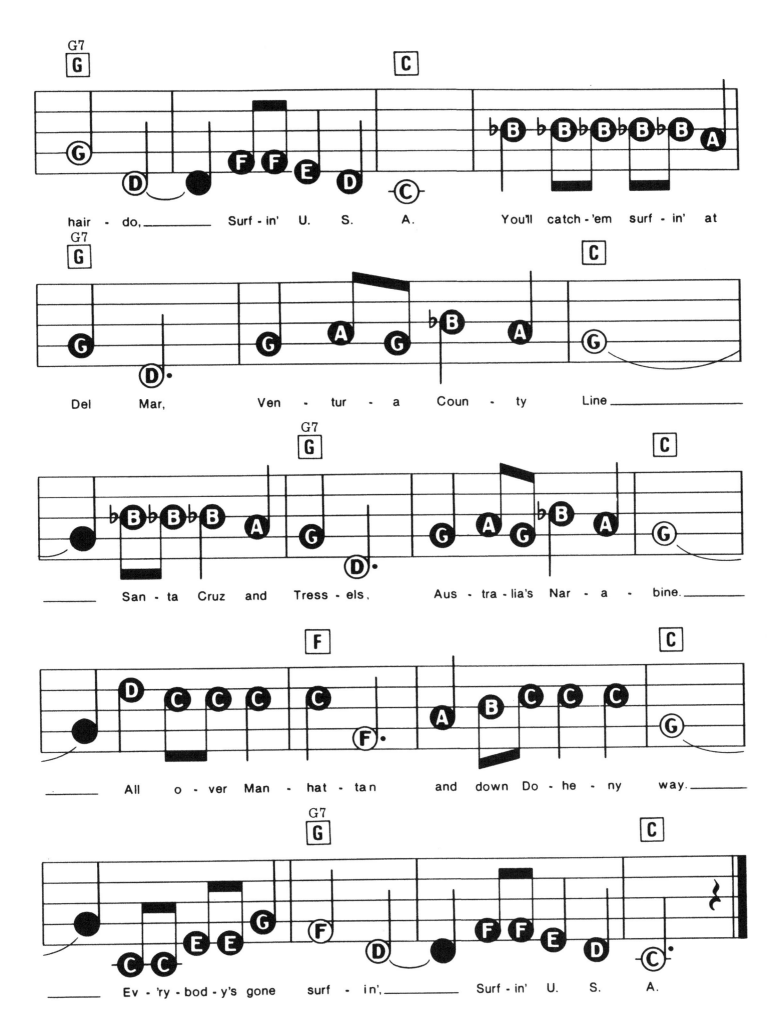

Tutti Frutti

Registration 4
Rhythm: Rock or 8 Beat

Words and Music by Little Richard Penniman
and Dorothy La Bostrie

The Twist

Registration 5
Rhythm: Rock

Words and Music by
Hank Ballard

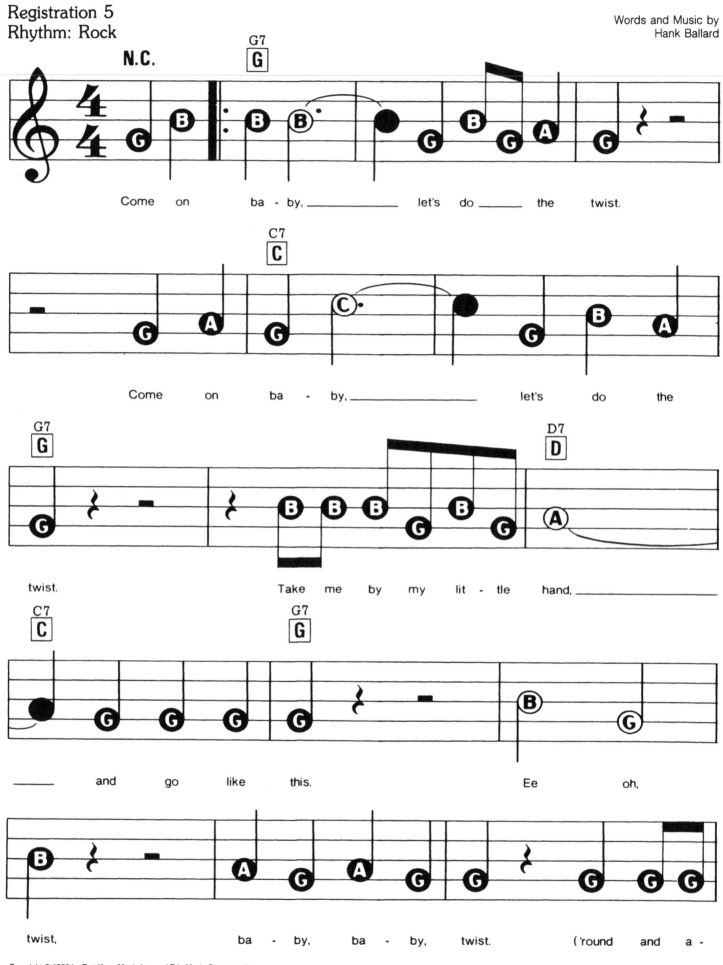

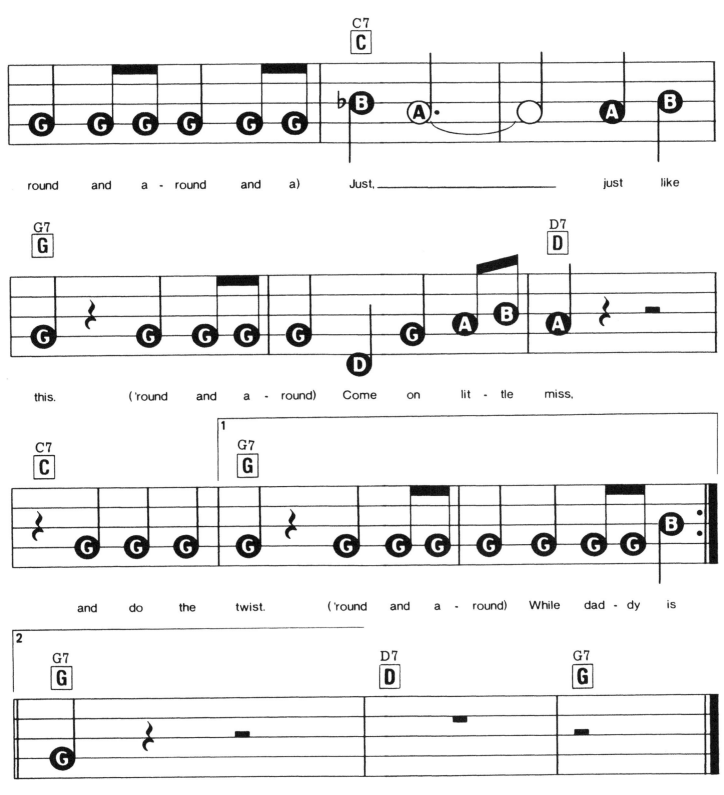

Verse 2
While daddy is sleeping and mama ain't around,
While daddy is sleeping and mama ain't around,
We're gonna twisty, twisty, twisty until we tear the house down.

You should see my little sis,
You should see my little sis,
She knows how to rock and she knows how to twist.

Yakety Yak

Registration 9
Rhythm: Rock or 8 Beat

Words and Music by Jerry Leiber
and Mike Stoller

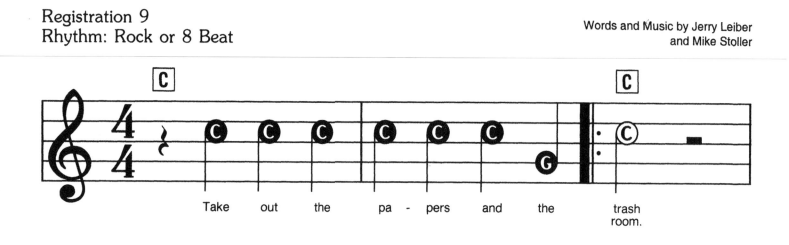

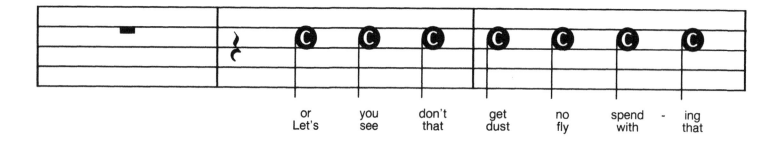

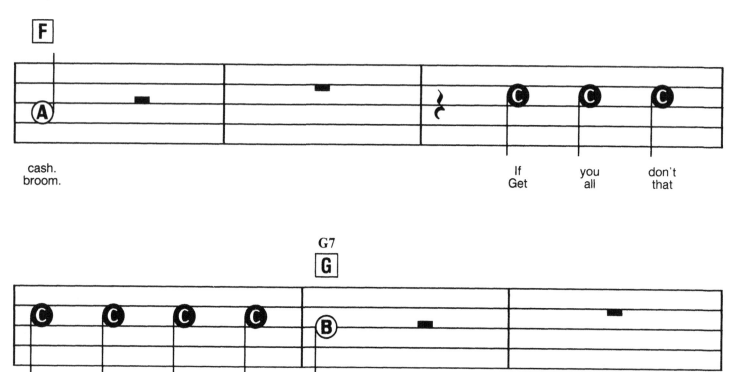

69

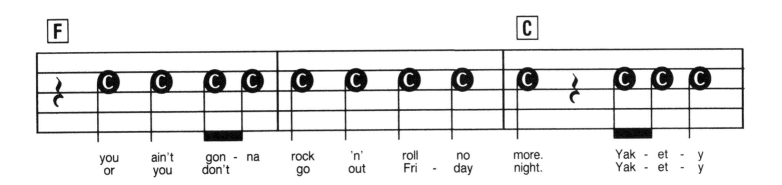

F ... **C**

you   ain't   gon - na   rock   'n'   roll   no   more.   Yak - et - y
or   you   don't   go   out   Fri - day   night.   Yak - et - y

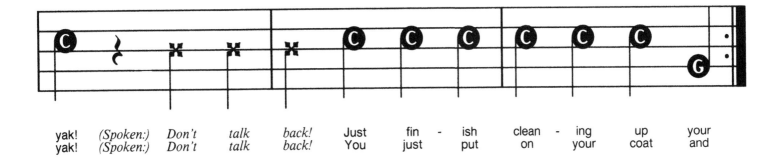

yak!   (Spoken:)   Don't   talk   back!   Just   fin - ish   clean - ing   up   your
yak!   (Spoken:)   Don't   talk   back!   You   just   put   on   your   coat   and

C

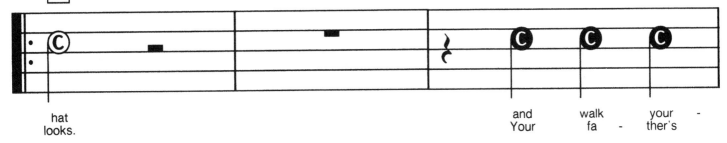

hat
looks.

and   walk   your -
Your   fa - ther's

F

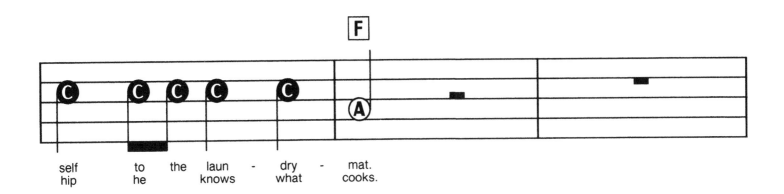

self   to   the   laun - dry - mat.
hip   he   knows   what   cooks.

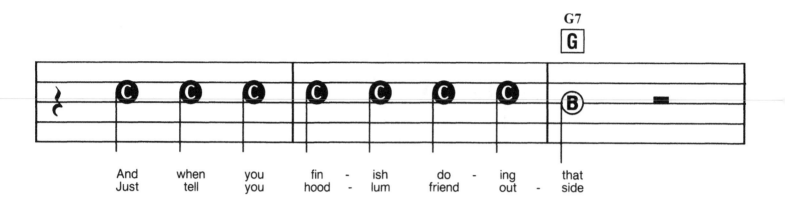

And when you fin - ish do - ing that
Just tell you hood - lum friend out - side

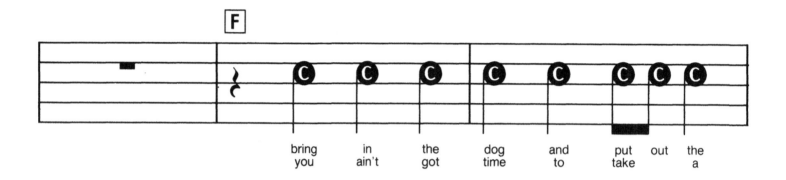

bring in the dog and put out the
you ain't got time to take a

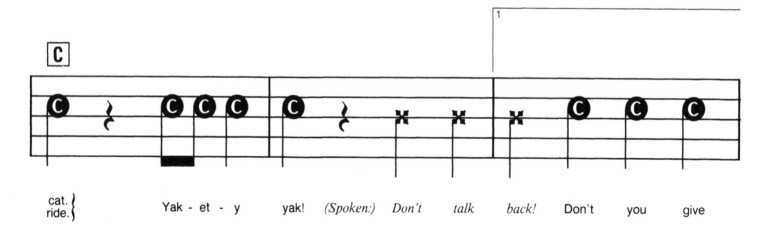

cat.
ride.
Yak - et - y yak! *(Spoken:) Don't talk back!* Don't you give

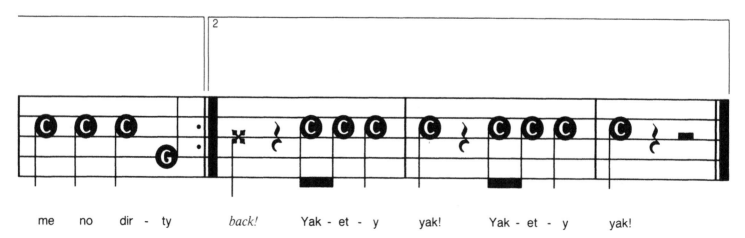

me no dir - ty *back!* Yak - et - y yak! Yak - et - y yak!

Registration Guide

- Match the Registration number on the song to the corresponding numbered category below. Select and activate an instrumental sound available on your instrument.

- Choose an automatic rhythm appropriate to the mood and style of the song. (Consult your Owner's Guide for proper operation of automatic rhythm features.)

- Adjust the tempo and volume controls to comfortable settings.

Registration

1	Mellow	Flutes, Clarinet, Oboe, Flugel Horn, Trombone, French Horn, Organ Flutes
2	Ensemble	Brass Section, Sax Section, Wind Ensemble, Full Organ, Theater Organ
3	Strings	Violin, Viola, Cello, Fiddle, String Ensemble, Pizzicato, Organ Strings
4	Guitars	Acoustic/Electric Guitars, Banjo, Mandolin, Dulcimer, Ukulele, Hawaiian Guitar
5	Mallets	Vibraphone, Marimba, Xylophone, Steel Drums, Bells, Celesta, Chimes
6	Liturgical	Pipe Organ, Hand Bells, Vocal Ensemble, Choir, Organ Flutes
7	Bright	Saxophones, Trumpet, Mute Trumpet, Synth Leads, Jazz/Gospel Organs
8	Piano	Piano, Electric Piano, Honky Tonk Piano, Harpsichord, Clavi
9	Novelty	Melodic Percussion, Wah Trumpet, Synth, Whistle, Kazoo, Perc. Organ
10	Bellows	Accordion, French Accordion, Mussette, Harmonica, Pump Organ, Bagpipes